The Struggle for Virtue

The Struggle for Virtue

Asceticism in a Modern Secular Society

Archbishop Averky (Taushev)

Holy Trinity Publications
The Printshop of St Job of Pochaev
Holy Trinity Monastery
Jordanville, New York

Printed with the blessing of His Eminence,
Metropolitan Hilarion, First Hierarch
of the Russian Orthodox Church Outside of Russia

The Struggle for Virtue: Asceticism in a Modern Secular Society
© 2014 Holy Trinity Monastery

HOLY TRINITY PUBLICATIONS
The Printshop of St Job of Pochaev
Holy Trinity Monastery
Jordanville, New York 13361-0036
www.holytrinitypublications.com

These lectures formed part of a Russian-language book titled
Современность и духовная жизнь
(Jordanville, N.Y.: Holy Trinity Monastery, 2006)
ISBN 9780884650942

ISBN: 978-0-88465-373-8 (paperback)
ISBN: 978-0-88465-374-5 (ePub)
ISBN: 978-0-88465-375-2 (Kindle)
Library of Congress Control Number: 2014937217

CONTENTS

Preface		vii
Introduction: The Essence and Meaning of Asceticism		ix
1. Self-Asserting Pride and Christian Humility		1
2. The Importance of Spiritual Discernment		18
3. Gospel Love and Humanistic Altruism		32
4. Acquiring Gospel Love		48
5. Reawakening Our Conscience		61
6. The Christian Understanding of Freedom		71
7. Guarding the Heart Amidst the Distractions of Life		86
8. Resisting Evil		98
9. Waging Unseen Warfare		110
10. Christian Struggle		122
11. The Holy Fathers on Combating the Passions		127
12. Pastoral Asceticism		138
Notes		143
Subject Index		145
Scripture Index		167

Archbishop Averky (Taushev)

**The future Archbishop Averky
holding the Kursk Root Icon**

PREFACE

Archbishop Averky (Taushev) (1906–1976) was the fourth abbot of Holy Trinity Monastery in Jordanville, New York. He was born in Imperial Russia but had to leave the country with his family in the wake of the Russian Revolution. Living in Bulgaria, he was drawn to the monastic life and soon became a monk and a priest. He taught and ministered in Bulgaria, Czechoslovakia, Yugoslavia, and Germany before being assigned in 1951 to teach at the Holy Trinity Seminary. In 1952, he became its rector. He was consecrated a bishop and, after the death of Archbishop Vitaly (Maximenko) in 1960, he became the abbot of Holy Trinity Monastery. As abbot and rector, he was heavily involved in the formation of the seminary curriculum and the daily life of the seminarians and monks. He was praised by converts to the Orthodox faith, such as Hieromonk Seraphim (Rose), for being a steadfast defender of traditional Orthodoxy. Considered one of the real luminaries of the Russian Orthodox Church Outside of Russia, he wrote many commentaries on scripture and other works that are extensively read both in Russia and in the diaspora. He reposed on March 31/April 13, 1976.

In memory of the thirty-fifth anniversary of the blessed repose of His Eminence, Archbishop Averky, the journal *Orthodox Life* serialized thirteen lectures on moral theology and asceticism that he had delivered in Western Europe shortly after the end of the World War II. Now in the English language, they are brought together in this volume for the edification and encouragement of the reader. They have been edited for publication as a single work.

The reader should be aware that the translator and editors did not have access to the same editions of the Russian language books used by the author when he wrote his lectures. Furthermore, not all of these works exist in English translation, and where they do it is not always possible to cite a corresponding reference.

Additionally, the author followed a Russian cultural and intellectual practice in which it is not considered essential to give all details of the source material but simply an indication of its origins. Therefore, the bibliography and endnotes at the end of this English edition are listed to facilitate the reader's understanding or indicate as closely as possible a source for further reading and study.

INTRODUCTION

The Essence and Meaning of Asceticism

What is "asceticism"? What is an "ascetic"? Many secular people among the ranks of modern Christians know the words "ascetic" and "asceticism" by hearsay, but very few have a correct understanding of what these words mean and express. These words ordinarily bring about a kind of superstitious horror in modern people who consider themselves Christians but who live far from the spirit of the Church and who are alien to the Church and the spiritual life, being wholly given over to a secular life of distraction.

"Asceticism" in modern secular society is normally perceived as being something extraordinarily gloomy, almost sinister, forever removed from "normal" human life. Many understand asceticism to be a kind of fanatical monstrosity or self-torture, akin to walking barefoot over burning coals or to hanging oneself up by one's ribs—as is done, for example, by Indian yogis and fakirs, to general amazement.

Such a distorted and prejudiced attitude towards the notion of asceticism in modern society demonstrates how far modern Christians have departed from a correct understanding of evangelical doctrine, how far they have "grown worldly," and how alien their understanding has become to the authentic *spiritual* life to which our Saviour, the Lord Jesus Christ, called not certain selected, exceptional persons, but *all* Christians in general.

One encounters another conception of the expressions "ascetic" and "asceticism" in modern society—one closer to the truth, but still too shallow and superficial, far from reaching the full profundity of these understandings and therefore also essentially incorrect. This view is too one-sided, touching only one less important and less essential side, but leaving without proper attention *the most important thing*, the innermost essence of these understandings. So, for example, it is said of a thin person with a pale, haggard face, "He looks like a real ascetic," not at all thinking about why he is thin and has a pale face: from forced or voluntary hunger, from poor nourishment, or from taking upon himself the struggle of abstinence from food. It is not difficult to see how superficial such a judgment is, for it concerns only a person's appearance, how he looks outwardly, leaving without attention his inner constitution, his disposition of spirit. Normally "asceticism" is understood as self-restraint, the restriction of one's natural needs to the possible minimum, but without any thought of *why and for what reason* this is done; or one may think erroneously and incorrectly that such self-restraint is *an end in and of itself* for these people, who are some kind of eccentrics voluntarily refraining, for unknown reasons and purposes, from the natural and therefore lawful pleasures that man's bodily nature enjoys. One way or another, we do not encounter a correct understanding of asceticism in modern society. The sole reason for this is that modern society does not live a spiritual life. Someone who does not live a spiritual life will have a difficult time understanding the essence and meaning of asceticism. People who live according to the spirit of this world will never understand the meaning of asceticism, no matter how it is explained to them, but will always have a distorted or partial conception, one suffering from one-sidedness.

So what is asceticism?

Asceticism is something so closely bound up with the spiritual life that without it spiritual life is simply *inconceivable*. It is, so to speak, the primary instrument of spiritual life. It is by no means an end in and of itself, but only a means; nonetheless, it is an absolutely necessary means for success in spiritual life. In what does this means consist?

Spiritual life is born in man through faith in God and in His Revelation. However, *faith without works is dead* (Jas 2:26) and we, as the Apostle Paul testifies, are *created in Christ Jesus for good works, which God prepared beforehand that we should walk in them* (Eph 2:10). It goes without saying that good works are essential for success in the spiritual life, for they demonstrate the presence of good will in us, without which there is no moving forward; in turn, good works themselves strengthen, develop, and deepen this good will. Good will attracts God's grace, without which full and decisive success in the spiritual life is unattainable, as a consequence of the profound brokenness inflicted on human nature by sin. It follows that the striving to perform good works is a necessary undertaking for all who desire to live an authentic spiritual life. *Not everyone who says to Me, "Lord, Lord," shall enter the kingdom of heaven; but he who does the will of My Father in heaven* (Matt 7:21)—to this the Lord Jesus Christ Himself testifies. In His farewell discourse with His disciples at the Mystical Supper, He decisively stated this condition: *If you love Me, keep My commandments* (John 14:15).

Therefore, the fulfillment of the evangelical commandments, or the performing of good works, is an essential foundation for the spiritual life. One who disregards the fulfillment of the commandments and does not perform good works is alien to true spiritual life. However, the evil habits and sinful disposition of soul that live in us resist the fulfillment of the commandments and the performance of good works. Every time we would like to perform some good work, we must overcome and suppress in ourselves one evil habit or another that protests against the good work we would like to accomplish. In this manner, a battle emerges in the soul between good aspirations and evil habits.

Here is what has already long ago been ascertained by experience. The greater our good works, and the more often we perform them, the easier it becomes to overcome evil habits: they are weakened by the increased frequency of our good works and are less able to counteract our good will—which, to the contrary, is increasingly strengthened by good works. An obvious conclusion can be drawn from this: he who desires success in the spiritual life must by all possible means force himself to perform good works as often and as varied as possible. He must **constantly practice the performance of good works**—that is, works of love for God and works of love for one's neighbor, or such works as would demonstrate that we are indeed striving to love God and neighbor with true evangelical love.

This constant **practice of performing good works bears the name of "asceticism,"** and one who practices the performance of good works by forcing himself is called an "ascetic." Inasmuch as asceticism is the foundation of the spiritual life and its primary instrument, the science of the spiritual life is itself normally called **"askesis."**

It is now clear just how greatly the true understanding of asceticism differs from secular society's false understanding. Later on, we shall see where this false and distorted secular understanding of asceticism comes from. We have already said that the performance of good works is opposed by evil habits rooted in our soul and body. We must overcome and uproot these evil habits in ourselves, and this is sometimes altogether torturous and accompanied by suffering; this struggle can be quite painful. In any event, when this is expressed outwardly, someone who does not know or understand the spiritual life will indeed fail to comprehend why this is the case or with what intention the "ascetic" is torturing himself and causing himself suffering. Hence arises the false, distorted perception of asceticism as some kind of fanatical monstrosity or self-torture.

Meanwhile, as we have seen, it is above all the practice of performing good deeds, accompanied by the suppression of evil habits, that is called asceticism. The very philological interpretation of the word "asceticism" demonstrates that this is the case. This word comes from the Greek *askesis*, which in its original meaning meant simply "exercise"; later, it meant a "given way of life," "calling," "trade," "occupation," and finally, in its most removed meaning, "ascetic struggle," "spiritual life," and "monasticism." Therefore, the word "ascetic," having been derived from the Greek *askitis*, in no way implies a kind of superstitious fanatic occupying himself with self-torture for who knows what reason, as many secular people think. Instead, according to its original meaning, it means a "fighter," as is indicated by a very characteristic analogy used by St Paul in his first epistle to the Corinthians (9:24–27), comparing physical and spiritual exercises in the attainment of one's desired goal: a corruptible crown for physical fighters and an incorruptible crown for spiritual fighters. Further meanings of the word "ascetic" are "struggler," "one engaged in divine contemplation," "recluse," and "monk."

It follows that "asceticism" is nothing other than "spiritual exercise" or "spiritual training," if one may express it analogously with physical, bodily training, which is just as essential for those exercising on the spiritual field as bodily training is essential as those exercising on the field of physical contests.

What specifically does this spiritual training consist of?

It consists of continually forcing oneself to perform good works and to suppress the soul's evil habits and aspirations that resist them. This is no easy matter, inasmuch as it is accompanied by strenuous efforts and not infrequently by a martyric battle that the Holy Fathers and ascetics called, not without reason, self-crucifixion, in accordance with the words of St Paul: *And those who are Christ's have crucified the flesh with its passions and desires* (Gal 5:24). The great Apostle to the gentiles himself, referring to his own personal spiritual experience, speaks vividly and expressively of the difficulties of the battle: *For I know that in me (that is, in my flesh,) nothing good dwells: for to will is present with me; but how to perform what is good I do not find. For the good that I will to do, I do not do; but the evil I will not to do, that I practice. Now if I do what I will not to do, it is no longer I who do it, but sin that dwells in me. I find then a law, that evil is present with me, the one who wills to do good. For I delight in the law of God according to the inward man. But I see another law in my members, warring against the law of my mind, and bringing me into captivity to the law of sin which is in my members. O wretched man that I am! Who will deliver me from this body of death? I thank God—through Jesus Christ our Lord! So then, with the mind I myself serve the law of God, but with the flesh the law of sin* (Rom 7:18–25). This eternal duality in man came about when his once healthy nature was damaged by sin, which introduced disorder and disharmony into it. This constant opposition by the law of sin, which lodges in the flesh, **makes asceticism necessary**. The essence of asceticism consists in **constantly forcing oneself**, constantly making oneself to do not that which the sin living in us wants to do, but rather that which the law of God, the law of good, requires. Without this, it goes without saying, there can be no success in the spiritual life. The ascetic is one who forces himself to do everything that is conducive to growth and development in the spiritual life and does nothing that would prevent this. We have already seen that growth and development in the spiritual life allow the accomplishment of works of love in relation to God and in relation to one's neighbor. It is obvious that everything that prevents love of God and neighbor—that is, doing evil works, the opposite of good—impedes the spiritual life. It follows that the ascetic is one who constantly forces himself to perform good works and to refrain from evil works.

But this is not yet everything. The goal of asceticism is far from exhausted by this alone. He who performs good works and refrains from evil works is not yet a full ascetic. Works alone, as such, are limited. Good works do not have power and significance in and of themselves, but only as an indication and external expression of a good disposition, a good aspiration of the soul, a visible affirmation of the presence of good will in us. After all, the Pharisee, too, performs good works, but they do not flow from a good disposition of soul in him, but from hypocrisy; that is, they flow from an evil disposition, and consequently, they do not testify to the presence of good aspirations in him. In precisely the same way, evil works, insofar as they are authentically evil, are dangerous and pernicious, inasmuch as they serve as the expression and external manifestation of the soul's evil aspirations, evil habits, and evil will. If there is no evil will, there will be no evil works. This means that the main thing is not works but **man's inner disposition**, the good or evil will of his soul and the virtuous or depraved condition of his heart, from which good or evil works are born naturally. Christ the Saviour Himself speaks of this clearly: ***But those things which proceed out of the mouth come from the heart, and they defile a man. For out of the heart proceed evil thoughts, murders, adulteries, fornications, thefts, false witness, blasphemies*** (Matt 15:18–19).

From this it is evident that the center of gravity in the spiritual life is not in works, as such, but in those dispositions of soul and that inner state of man from which they result. Therefore, for the true ascetic, it is far from sufficient only to refrain from evil works and only to perform good works: the true ascetic strives to uproot from his soul evil dispositions, evil habits, and evil will, and in their place to plant and firmly inculcate good dispositions, good habits, and good will. This is the primary labor—difficult to the point of drawing blood—or **struggle** of the true ascetic. The soul's evil habits do not easily give way to good habits: they fight fiercely for their predominance, for their reigning position in man's soul. Habits, having taken root through their frequent satisfaction, increase in strength, like natural qualities and properties of the soul: they are, as it were, innate to the soul. It is no wonder that the popular saying goes, "Habits are a second nature." Depraved habits are like shackles on a man: they deprive him of his moral freedom and keep him like a prisoner. The more one satisfies his depraved habits, the stronger they grow, making such a person into a pitiful, weak-willed slave. "Fear evil habits," says one of the greatest instructors of asceticism, St Isaac the Syrian, "*more than demons*." And, to the contrary, when one battles against them, they weaken more and more until they subside altogether. "A resolute determination," writes our native teacher of asceticism, Bishop Ignatius (Brianchaninov), "enlightened and strengthened by the grace of Christ, can overcome even the most deeply-rooted habits. . . . A habit initially fiercely resists one who wants to overthrow its yoke, seeming invincible at first; but in time, with constant battle against it, and with every act of disobedience to it, it grows weaker and weaker. . . . If in the course of battle it should happen to you that, due to some unexpected circumstance, you are defeated, *do not be troubled*, do not fall into hopelessness, but begin the battle anew."

In this way, we see that an unceasing battle between good and evil goes on in the soul of the ascetic. This unceasing battle with evil is called *"spiritual"* or *"unseen warfare"* in the spiritual or ascetic literature. This spiritual or unseen warfare is the very essence of asceticism or spiritual life.

What, then, is the final goal of asceticism and what is its meaning for success in the spiritual life?

Let us sum up all that has been said above.

The human soul, being divine in origin, always aspires towards God. It cannot find full satisfaction in anything earthly and, suffering severely in its alienation from God, it can find rest only in God. The human soul can attain this salvific communion with God only through the fulfillment of the commandments of love for God and neighbor. The commandments of love for God and neighbor can be fulfilled only through the uprooting of the "law of sin" living in us—evil habits and evil dispositions of soul—and through the planting in their place of good habits and good dispositions of soul. This does not happen without fierce battle or *struggle*. It is precisely this battle or struggle that is the essence of asceticism, which makes possible man's success in the spiritual life—that is, in drawing near to God and entering into communion with God, for which the human spirit longs. It is from this battle, or struggle, that asceticism itself bears the name "struggle," that the spiritual life is called the "life of struggle," and that those who live the ascetic life are also called "strugglers." "Struggling"[1] is a purely Russian word that fully corresponds in spirit to the meaning of the Greek word "asceticism."

Should everyone, all Christians, be ascetic strugglers?

This question is tantamount to asking: is everyone created by God and destined by Him for the spiritual life and spiritual communion with their Creator?

Modern human society, which on the whole neither lives the spiritual life nor desires to know anything about it, but lives only a corporeal life, shuns spiritual struggle; it does not understand it and therefore even fears the very word "asceticism," distorting its meaning, as we mentioned at the beginning. Normally, modern people—even among those who consider themselves Christians—feel that spiritual struggle and asceticism is the lot of certain exceptional persons and is required only for monastics, who have specially dedicated themselves to a life of struggle and asceticism. "We are not monks; this is not required of us"—this is how modern secular people normally answer the call to live the spiritual life and to begin the battle against their sinful, evil habits.

Of course, no one would deny that it is primarily monks who take upon themselves the obligation of living the spiritual life and of being ascetic strugglers. But can laymen, who have not given monastic vows, consider themselves wholly free from such an obligation? Only through incomprehension, thoughtlessness, and a misunderstanding of that to which God calls all Christians, regardless of whether they are monks or laymen.

After all, what essentially distinguishes monks from laymen?

Only that, in the words of that great teacher of monasticism, Abba Dorotheus, "they understood that they could not conveniently perform the virtues while living in the world and therefore contrived a particular way of life, a particular way of spending time, and a particular manner of behaving" (*First Discourse*).

The difference, it follows, consists only in the *external* forms of life: monks developed for themselves more convenient external forms of life in order more easily and without hindrance to attain the goal of human life, common to all: communion with God. Thus, in particular, monks freed themselves from all worldly ties, concerns, and cares—such as, for instance, family life and the possession of property— exclusively in order to engage in spiritual warfare more freely and to overcome and uproot the evil habits preventing them from acquiring evangelical love for God and neighbor more easily. However, the spirit of life for both monks and laypeople—as follows perfectly clearly from everything that has been said above—must be, of course, *one and the same.*

Could it be that God created monks and laypeople separately? Could it be that God breathed the breath of life only into the faces of monks, leaving laypeople like mute animals? Could it be that only the spirits of monks strive for God, seeking communion with Him, while laypeople are not called to a life in God? Could it be that only monks have inherited a nature damaged by the ancestral sin and therefore must battle against sinful habits? Could it be that the Lord Jesus Christ, our Saviour, came to earth only for monks, and not for everyone? Could it be that He founded His Church, in which grace-filled power is given for overcoming the law of sin and evil habits, for monks alone? Could it be that the Gospel was written only for monks alone? Could it be that the Lord calls them alone, and not everyone, to His eternal, blessed Kingdom to come?

Who would dare claim this? To say this would be to reveal a completely ossified soul, a total and profound ignorance, and a hopeless misunderstanding of the meaning of human life! Would anyone claim that monks alone suffer from the reign of sinful passions in the world, the result of evil habits, and not everyone without exception? This means that *everyone*, without any exception whatsoever, is equally called to battle with sinful passions and evil habits in order to free themselves from the oppression of the power of evil reigning in the world and ruthlessly terrorizing everyone, as we observe so clearly in the present time. It is clear that everyone, if he desires to save himself from this oppressing power of evil, must enter the path of the spiritual life—that is, to become an ascetic struggler to some extent. One who avoids this is doomed to perdition.

Asceticism is for everyone, not for monks alone, for it is by no means in opposition to nature, as some think, or a kind of coercion thrust upon man. The opposite is the case: it is a natural requirement of the human spirit—which strives to free itself from the oppressing power of evil and to soar toward its First Cause, God—to find in Him the fullest satisfaction of all his inner strivings and needs and to obtain the happiness, peace, joy, and eternal rest so longed for by everyone. Asceticism alone, which unites man with

God, the Source and Giver of all good things, is the true path to that inviting beacon of happiness to which everyone living on this earth so impetuously strives. How often people, pursuing happiness, perish both in this earthly life and, what is particularly terrible, in the future, eternal life! For happiness, as life experience demonstrates, is not outside man, where he mistakenly looks for it, but *inside* him: happiness is in the peaceful arrangement of the soul, in the serene inner peace that is the consequence of the deep inner satisfaction that comes as a result of conquering evil after uprooting the evil habits that tyrannize the soul. No one can ever be happy when sinful passions and evil and depraved habits, which will always bring about confusion and chaos, reign in the soul. The only way to pacify the soul is to suppress and uproot evil habits—that is, through asceticism, the ascetic way of life.

This is why asceticism, to one degree or another, is without doubt essential for everyone without exception: it is a *common* good, a common property. One who shuns asceticism is his own enemy, depriving himself of the highest good: peace of conscience and blessed communion with God.

Asceticism is not simply some human invention, displeasing to God, as certain enemies of the ascetic life would seek to affirm. On the contrary, it is the only trustworthy and reliable means for realizing the clear and direct will of God for man. As for what this will of God is for man, it is clearly expressed in the compelling words of the incarnate Son of God Himself, our Lord Jesus Christ, in the so-called Sermon on the Mount. These words do not permit misinterpretation: **Therefore you shall be perfect, just as your Father in heaven is perfect** (Matt 5:48). According to the design of God Himself, Who created man, the lofty final goal of all the aspirations of a Christian who battles against his sinful passions and evil habits is *likeness to God*. What is this perfection to which the Lord calls us to aspire? In what must we endeavor to be likened to God? There is a direct and clear indication in the Word of God: **Be holy, for I am holy** (1 Pet 1:16), said the Lord. The Apostle Paul, in his epistle to the Thessalonians, asserts just as categorically: **For this is the will of God, your sanctification** (1 Thess 4:3).

As such, there can be no doubt; everything is clear. The Lord expects perfection, which consists of holiness akin to the holiness of God, from everyone created by Him (and not only monks). This is the clear and defined will of God, and now it depends on us either to fulfill this will of God or to resist it. Holiness resists sin, which is overcome only by an ascetic life. It follows that asceticism, which uproots sin and thereby leads man to holiness, is not an unnecessary human invention; it is a powerful means indicated by God Himself for the attainment by man of God's will for him. One who opposes the ascetic life, it goes without saying, is an opponent of the will of God and an enemy of God.

God created us to be holy, as He is holy, to be blissful, and to delight in a communion of love with Him. We departed from God's plan when our forefather fell into sin. Sin separated us from God, making us deeply unhappy. The life of struggle or asceticism repairs evil, the cause of sin: it returns us to blessed communion with God. Blessed love, desiring our salvation, waits for us all to enter onto this only saving path of ascetic life and, on it, to find eternal, blessed communion with God, in Whom alone is the full and perfect satisfaction of the human soul's loftiest needs and requirements.

CHAPTER 1

Self-Asserting Pride and Christian Humility

Beloved, do not believe every spirit, but test the spirits, whether they are of God; because many false prophets have gone out into the world. By this you know the Spirit of God: Every spirit that confesses that Jesus Christ has come in the flesh is of God, and every spirit that does not confess that Jesus Christ has come in the flesh is not of God. And this is the spirit of the Antichrist, which you have heard was coming; and is now already in the world. (1 John 4:1–3)

If such a warning by the beloved disciple of Christ, the Holy Apostle and Evangelist John the Theologian, was necessary in apostolic times, then it is all the more timely now. For it is unlikely that at any time in human history have so many false prophets captivated people with the specter of good as now, in our times. If we approach this spirit with the standard indicated by the Apostle, then it can be shown that they "do not confess that Jesus Christ is come in the flesh," even if certain of them do not display open hostility to our Lord and Saviour.

So what was the essence of the sin of Adam and Eve?

It was that they questioned the all-good God the Creator and put more faith in the devil, the enemy of God, than in God, thereby breaking God's commandment and wishing to become gods themselves knowing good and evil.

And he said to the woman, "Has God indeed said, 'You shall not eat of every tree of the garden'?" And the woman said to the serpent, "We may eat the fruit of the trees of the garden; but of the fruit of the tree which is in the midst of the garden, God has said, 'You shall not eat it, nor shall you touch it, lest you die.'" Then the serpent said to the woman, "You will not surely die. For God knows that in the day you eat of it your eyes will be opened, and you will be like God, knowing good and evil." So when the woman saw that the tree was good for food, that it was pleasant to the eyes, and a tree desirable to make one wise, she took of its fruit and ate. She also gave to her husband with her, and he ate. Then the eyes of both of them were opened, and they knew that they were naked; and they sewed fig leaves together and made themselves coverings. (Gen 3:1–7)

Therefore, the essence of our primogenitors' sin was that they did not want to obey God, but rather desired to become gods themselves. The devil, in seducing them, communicated to them that same spirit of self-asserting pride that had been the cause of his own fall. The spirit of self-asserting human pride, and with it protest against the all-good will of God, has ever since become rooted in people's souls and has become the cause of mankind's infection with sin and sinful corruption. We can find its footprints throughout the entire history of mankind.

It was precisely this spirit of self-asserting human pride that was the cause of the first war: the fratricide performed by Cain, who was envious of his brother Abel. This awful sin of fratricide led mankind to such a hopeless situation of complete depravity that the Lord had to have recourse to as radical a means of suppressing the spread of sin as the universal flood. Yet sinful corruption made itself known again in Noah's descendants who survived the flood. His son Ham, whose name became a byword, became a striking example of disrespect to parents and of rejection of parental authority—the source of which was rooted, of course, in that same self-affirming human pride that induces one to act condescendingly, contemptuously, scornfully, and sarcastically towards other people, even if they are older and worthy of the respect due to their position.

It was this same human pride that induced people, for the sake of "making a name for themselves," to begin construction of the Tower of Babel, which prompted God to counteract against human pride by confusing the tongues, after which people dispersed over all the earth and formed various nations, among whom there has been constant warfare ever since. As such, pride has engendered division among people, making them alien and hostile towards one another.

Dispersed all over the world, people became divided into different tribes and nations; all the while, at the foundation of this division lay that very same self-asserting human pride in the form of so-called national pride. This has given birth to embittered enmity between different nations and the countless wars with which human history is filled, giving the impression, if one opens any modern textbook of history, that the entire history of the human race is essentially a history of war: one war succeeds another—and that is all there is to it. It makes perfect sense that mankind, having lost its unity and having been divided into many nations warring against one another, would have therewith lost faith in the One God and knowledge of the oneness of the Divinity. Every nation came to have its own national gods that corresponded to its spirit and tastes. Every nation reflected its own national character in its religion, creating gods "in its own image." Such is the origin of paganism, that perverted religion created as the result of that same spirit of self-asserting human pride. This oblivion to the One True God and worship of false gods created by man's imagination "in his own image," this idolization of his own passions and vices, became the occasion for a profound moral fall, into the abyss of which the ancient world descended ever more deeply before the coming of Christ.

The Apostle Paul speaks eloquently of this in his Epistle to the Romans: *And even as they did not like to retain God in their knowledge, God gave them over to a debased mind, to do these things which are not fitting; being filled with all unrighteousness, sexual immorality, wickedness, covetousness, maliciousness; full of envy, murder, strife, deceit, evil-mindedness; they are whisperers, backbiters, haters of God, violent, proud, boasters, inventors of evil things, disobedient to parents, undiscerning, untrustworthy, unloving, unforgiving, unmerciful* (Rom 1:28–31).

When evil had reached its highest strain on earth, when mankind through its limitless fall had reached a complete moral impasse, then the "great mystery of Godliness" was accomplished: God sent His Only-Begotten Son to earth to save the perishing human world. How did the Son of God, having come to earth, heal fallen mankind? Naturally, with the very medicine that was capable of healing man's primary disease. Mankind, as we have seen, was sick with pride—so the Lord healed it with humility. The Lord teaches this lesson of humility not only through His preaching, but above all through His own example—the example of His earthly life, beginning with His very birth.

Where was the Lord born? Neither in a rich home nor in a luxurious palace, but in a poor cave; not in Rome, the capital of the world in those days, but in the scorned, pitiful, and poor land of Judea. Where did the Lord live? He lived, in His own words, having *nowhere to lay His head* (Luke 9:58). How did His life on earth end? Shamefully, in the eyes of society back then, executed on a cross like the endmost criminal. Celsus, a famous enemy and opponent of Christianity, wrote: "His life was most reprehensible, and His death was most miserable." Having given His own life as an example of the most profound humility, the incarnate Only-Begotten Son of God also lay humility as the foundation of His teaching. *From that time Jesus began to preach and to say, "Repent, for the kingdom of heaven is at hand"* (Matt 4:17). "Repent"— that is, lay aside your pride, acknowledge yourself as a sinner, and hasten to God not with a feeling of self-satisfied superiority, but with the feeling of your spiritual poverty, your nothingness, your indecency, and pray to God for the forgiveness of your sins and for mercy. He began His Sermon on the Mount by glorifying the *poor in spirit*, that is, the humble: *Blessed are the poor in spirit, for theirs is the kingdom of heaven* (Matt 5:3). Calling to Himself in particular all that *labor and are heavy laden*, as being the most capable of acquiring the virtue of humility, He says to them, *Take My yoke upon you and learn from Me, for I am gentle and lowly in heart, and you will find rest for your souls* (Matt 11:29). He also taught His Apostles humility, cutting short in them all pretensions and strivings for precedence by saying to them more than once: *Whosoever desires to be great among you, let him be your servant* (Matt 20:26).

According to the Lord's words, those who desire to enter the Kingdom of God must humble themselves like little children. *At that time the disciples came to Jesus, saying, "Who then is greatest in the kingdom of heaven?" Then Jesus called a little child to Him, set him in the midst of them, and said, "Assuredly, I say to you, unless you are converted and become as little children, you will by no means enter the kingdom of heaven* (Matt 18:1–3).

At the Mystical Supper, wishing once again to emphasize the necessity of humility for His followers, the Lord washed the feet of His disciples, saying: *Do you know what I have done to you? You call me Teacher and Lord: and you say well, for so I am. If I then, your Lord and Teacher, have washed your feet, you also ought to wash one another's feet. For I have given you an example, that you should do as I have done to you* (John 13:12–15).

Such, then, is the "spirit of Christ"! The spirit of Christ is the spirit of humility, the antithesis of the spirit of self-asserting human pride. *Learn from Me, for I am gentle and lowly in heart* (Matt 11:29)—these words should be the life's motto of every Christian. *Let this mind be in you,* writes the Apostle Paul, *which was also in Christ Jesus* (Phil 2:5). What is this "mind"? This is what: *Who, being in the form of God, did not consider it robbery to be equal with God, but made Himself of no reputation, taking the form of a bondservant, and coming in the likeness of men. And being found in appearance as a man, He humbled Himself and became obedient to the point of death, even the death of the cross* (Phil 2:6–8). But you will say—and, indeed, many have said this and continue to say this—what good is there in the spirit of weakness, feebleness, poverty, and powerlessness? Is it not better, is it not more important, to have boldness, energy, and confidence in oneself and one's powers in life? Many do just that: the Christian teaching of humility is antithetical to the doctrine of the strong personality that battles persistently and overcomes all obstacles. Such, for example, was the teaching of the German philosopher Nietzsche concerning the *Übermensch*. He, like many others, considered Christian humility a form of weakness. But this is a mistake, a gross misunderstanding of the facts. Christian humility is not in any way a form of weakness, but just the opposite: it is strength in a person, although not human strength, but rather God's strength. *My strength is made perfect in weakness*, said the Lord to the Apostle Paul when the latter asked the Lord that the messenger of Satan that was buffeting him depart from him (2 Cor 12:9). Therefore, the Holy Apostle, understanding the significance of the Lord's words, said: *Most gladly I will rather boast in my infirmities, that the power of Christ may rest upon me* (2 Cor 12:9). Man has free will, and therefore the grace or power of God is fully manifested in him only when he wholly gives himself over to God, that is, when he is permeated with the spirit of humility and obedience to God's will. Human pride, however, thinking that it can cope through its own powers alone, interferes with the manifestation of God's power in man. Therefore, a humble person is not weak, but actually strong, because God's power manifests itself and acts through him; the proud man is weak, for he rejects God's all-powerful grace and is left with only his human powers, which are, of course, immeasurably weaker and less significant than God's all-powerful grace. Therefore, pride always sooner or later disgraces itself, and the proud man falls, perishing with all his self-confidence, plans, and calculations. In this way, in order to rectify our primogenitors' fall into sin, which had poisoned all mankind with the poison of pride and disobedience, the Lord Jesus Christ taught, and demonstrated by the example of His own life, humility, and obedience to the will of God. The ideal of humility and obedience has since then become the ideal for the new Christian mankind, renewed by the Lord Christ. However, the spirit of self-asserting pride, which had already taken root in people's souls, did not want to give way to the spirit of Christ. A terrible battle began, a bloody battle, not against life, but against death. For more than two centuries, Christians—those meek and humble followers of Christ's teaching—were martyred and tortured by pagans, who handed them over to horrible, unheard-of punishments. What was the ultimate result? From the point of view of those who consider humility to be a manifestation of weakness, one should have expected that all Christians would have been exterminated and that Christianity would have disappeared from the face of the earth. Yet just the opposite happened. The meek sheep of Christ's flock transformed the wolfish wrath of their persecutors into the meekness of lambs. Christianity did not disappear; on the contrary, paganism ceded its place to it. Christianity was victorious over paganism, becoming the reigning religious confession of the entire civilized world of that time. Is it not obvious that the truth of the following words has been borne out: *My strength is made perfect in weakness* (2 Cor 12:9)?

The spirit of self-asserting pride, however, did not cede its place conclusively. It found a place for itself in the hearts of those who had become Christians but had not fully assimilated the spirit of Christian humility. Disagreement began to appear in Christian society in the form of false teachings, in the so-called heresies and schisms. What was the origin of the heresies that especially shook the Church in the period from the fourth to the sixth centuries? Naturally, the same self-asserting human pride. One of the most horrible and dangerous heresies for the Church was Arianism, which denied the consubstantiality of the Son of God with God the Father and, as a consequence, negated Christianity. It owed its origins to Arius, a presbyter of Alexandria, who began preaching his new false teaching, which he had concocted himself, because he was offended that he had been overlooked when the new Archbishop of Alexandria was chosen. But the motives for the rise of a heresy are not always so crude; very often they are extremely subtle. Very subtle spiritual pride, self-opinion, and vainglory—almost unnoticeable to the person himself—can be produced by an ascetic life that lacks the spirit of true humility. It very often compels one to preach one's own new teaching, which contradicts the Church's teaching, because it springs from an unclean source: a soul contaminated by the spirit of pride and self-opinion. This explains why heretics were people who seemed to lead lofty ascetic lives, fasters and ascetics—such as, for example, Patriarch Nestorius of Constantinople, founder of the so-called "Nestorian" heresy.

The spirit of self-asserting human pride brought about, finally, a frightful and disastrous schism within the very heart of the Christian Church. The entire Western Roman Church, with its patriarch-pope at its head, fell away from ecclesial unity. And in turn Protestantism, with its numberless multitude of assorted branches or so-called sects, separated itself from it as well. Where do the roots of this schism lie? The causes are all too clear and obvious to any observant and thoughtful historian. The western world with Rome reigning at its head, before which all the nations of the world once trembled, demonstrated that it was incapable of properly assimilating and absorbing the spirit of Christian humility; pagan pride, love of authority, and the unquenchable thirst to rule and command continued to live even in Christian Rome, which had adopted the teaching of Christ superficially and shallowly. This spirit of pagan pride expressed itself in the pretensions of the Roman patriarch-pope to rule the entire Christian world. The pope continued the tradition of the pagan emperors of Rome, becoming as it were a successor to their politics of subjecting all nations under them. They forgot Christ's testimony to His Apostles: *Whosoever desires to become great among you, let him be your servant* (Matt 20:26). The pope placed himself above all other bishops, and pronounced his pretension to be the head of the entire Christian Church. This sad schism took place on July 16, 1054.

Having cut itself off from ecclesial unity, the entire Western Church, in the persons of its hierarchy, morally fell so profoundly that it provoked a protest headed by Luther and, later, Zwingli and Calvin. A new and frightful schism took place in the heart of Roman Catholicism itself, under the general name of Protestantism. Proudly renouncing the Church and its authority to interpret Holy Scripture and recognizing man himself as the sole authority—once again, that same spirit of self-asserting pride—Protestantism gave birth to a countless number of the most varied sects. As a result, we see the lamentable picture of the once united Church of Christ being divided into many different mutually hostile confessions. This is where that pernicious spirit of self-asserting human pride has led!

Regardless of heresies and schisms, Christ's saving teaching has nevertheless produced a rich harvest in people's hearts, and all human culture created under the salutary influence of the idea of Christ's teaching can justly be called Christian culture. Both science and art developed for many years under the Church's protection, not cutting ties with the Christian religion that had stimulated, inspired, and ennobled them. This continued until the end of the fifteenth and beginning of the sixteenth centuries, until the epoch of so-called humanism or the Renaissance. Then, under the influence of the brilliant flowering of science and art, many heads were turned, and the spirit of self-asserting human pride began decisively to displace the spirit of Christian humility. The epoch of "humanism" or the "Renaissance," which proclaimed the cult of the satiated, healthy, beautiful human flesh, was essentially humanity's renunciation of Christianity and a return to pagan ideals. Science and art "secularized"—that is, they became entirely "worldly," developing along the lines of autonomy and independence from the faith and the Church; they began more frequently to speak against the Church's teaching, opposing the spirit of humility and obedience with the spirit of self-opinion, self-assuredness, and the idolization of human reason. The cult of reason, as the highest criterion in life, thenceforward became firmly established; it even found outward expression, albeit a theatrical and sham one, during the French Revolution. Self-asserting human pride increasingly raised its head. Man stepped away from God, boldly denying His divine authority, and even began to deny God's very existence and to proclaim himself god. The divine-human Christian religion was replaced by man-deifying humanism. Indoctrinated in pride, self-opinion, and self-confidence in one's powers, abilities, and unlimited possibilities, man stopped striving towards spiritual perfection, towards his "deification," inasmuch as he saw himself perfect even without this, being like God and knowing good and evil. This rebirth of the primordial sin in all its power within human society led man increasingly to greater degrees of spiritual decline and moral depravity. If man is his own highest authority, and if he is not just man but "man-god"—for whom everything is permitted, for whom there are no barriers, and for whom everything is possible—then, of course, all manifestations of the passions and all means of pleasing the flesh are lawful to him. Serving the flesh comes first, in consequence of which one's spiritual needs are increasingly deadened and trampled upon; finally, in order to put the voice of the conscience living in one's spirit to an end once and for all, the very spirit is declared nonexistent. There is no spirit; there is only one material: the flesh, requiring satiation—such is the foundational position of the new epoch, the epoch of materialism. Materialism is the natural offspring and logical development of humanism. The ideal of the full stomach, concealed behind the loud names of the "ideal of social justice" and "social truth," became the highest ideal for a mankind that had renounced Christianity. The doctrine of socialism and Marxism-communism naturally grew from the ground of materialism. Humanism and materialism, by denying man's spiritual foundation and proclaiming him as god, thereby legitimatized the self-asserting human pride and animal egoism they naturally engendered. The constant conflict of interests among egoists resulted in human life becoming more complicated. Life became worse and more difficult, for the ceaseless and embittered battle between people's egotistical interests became the law of life. Everyone began to think only about himself, seeking his advantage alone, and to strive towards his own narrowly egotistical prosperity. What was the result? Those who were stronger, wealthier, and more cunning began to oppress and abuse those were weaker, poorer, and less cunning. So-called social evil arose; "social injustice" and "social ills" increased and magnified. Where was one to look for salvation from these social evils, how was one to establish social equality, so that everyone could live equally well and no one would offend or oppress anyone else? The only foundation for restraining people's passions is the law of Christ, which commands: *Bear ye one another's burdens* (Gal 6:2); *not to please ourselves*

(Rom 15:1); *And just as you want men to do to you, do you also do to them likewise* (Luke 6:31); and *You shall love your neighbor as yourself* (Mark 12:31). But this law of Christ was banished from life. Yet, inasmuch as life had become unlivable as a consequence of the increasing egoism and violence of some against others, something had to be invented in order to be freed from this evil and to establish a single way of life that was fair for all.

It did not enter anyone's head, however, that the root of this evil was the turning away from the "spirit of Christ," and replacing it with another "spirit," a *spirit that does not confess that Jesus Christ has come in the flesh* (1 John 4:3), a spirit that became the reigning orientation of human life: the spirit of self-asserting human pride. And so socialism and, later, its extreme manifestation, communism, became popular doctrines, new "spirits" of the last times, promising people liberation from all "social injustices" and the establishment of a peaceful, serene, genuinely paradisiacal life on earth, with happiness and contentment for all. But the problem was that these doctrines attempted to treat humanity's plagues with negative means. They neither saw nor understood that modern evil is rooted in the depths of the human soul, that mutual grievances and oppression came from the fact that people had renounced the "spirit of Christian meekness and humility," and had become hard-hearted egoists due to the growth and intensification in their souls of the "spirit of self-asserting human pride." They naively thought that all evil came from imperfect (in their opinion) governmental and social structures and that it would be enough to change these in order immediately to establish general prosperity on earth, with life becoming "paradise." Moreover, for the more extreme socialists, such as the communists, the change of structure necessary to attain this prosperity required violent means, including the shedding of blood and the physical destruction of those who did not agree with their doctrine. In other words, they thought they could conquer evil with evil, and frequently more bitter and unjust evil at that. Their mistake was that, wishing to overcome evil, which was the offspring of self-asserting human pride, they continued to consider that very same self-asserting human pride as their only faithful weapon in the battle. In this way, like a snowball, it grew inordinately, crushing more and more people under itself. It is clear that they could have no success; they led mankind into even more bitter evil and into an even more disastrous condition. You and I are now living witnesses of how all the utopian dreams of idealistic socialists and communists have collapsed, and how their efforts to establish a paradisiacal and happy life on earth resulted in mankind finding itself in an impassable moral dead-end; life became not paradise but real hell. Human pride run rampant led to each person's life losing all value and literally hanging on a string; the precious fruits of age-old culture were ruthlessly destroyed; and over it all hangs the specter of destruction of not only all of mankind, but even of our entire planet.

This is where the spirit of self-asserting human pride has led us, along with that "new faith" that has been persistently propagandized among us in recent years in place of the Christian faith, this "faith in oneself" and "faith in one's own god" rather than in the One True God. And just how persistently, obstinately, and artificially this pernicious faith has been propagandized is witnessed by something, seemingly insignificant at first glance, that I found in a book published in pre-war[1] Yugoslavia. It is the following unusually telling poem by Anton Aškerc entitled "Faith in Oneself":

Believe in your god,
believe in yourself,
god lives in our breast.
In our souls
he burns,
through our veins
our god spreads,
our god –
is our might and will.
This god is the one . . . who holds sway
from a sunny peak.
Believe in yourself! That is
in unworldly Ahasuerus –
the great new faith!

Is it not the case that this is a remarkably bold hymn of self-asserting human pride? Moreover, it is of limitless value to us as an open admission that the "new faith," which will replace and supplant the Christian faith, is the "faith of the unworldly Ahasuerus."

It is this genuine faith of the Antichrist that, as we have seen, has now born such disastrous fruits and has trodden mankind into an impassable moral dead end; it is persistently and tenaciously propagandized among us in society by all means and methods; it is fostered, sometimes quite successfully, in our youth, in the majority of our schools, and in various youth organizations and circles. This proud faith, alien to the spirit of Christian humility, in oneself and in "one's god," has engendered those apocalyptic horrors that we have just lived through; it also threatens us, through the even more perilous signs that hang above us, with a somber and cheerless future. This future for mankind is, I repeat, indisputably somber and cheerless, inasmuch as there is no evidence of a sobering up among people and no desire to return to the uniquely saving spirit of Christ—the spirit of meekness and humility. Only hope in God's mercy, which can affect mankind to sober up and come to its senses, can inspire in us the energy for life; for, without this hope, life would not be worth it, for it is obvious, especially after everything that we have experienced, that mankind can go no further along the path it has hitherto travelled, for horrible, inevitable perdition awaits us all on this path, as the natural reckoning for the sins of apostasy and of replacing the spirit of Christ with the spirit of the Antichrist.

The only spirit acceptable to us now is the spirit that confesses that Jesus Christ is come in the flesh; and if we have not entirely lost our minds and do not desire to perish utterly, we need to imitate the path of the Holy Apostle Paul, who said: *For I determined not to know anything among you except Jesus Christ and Him crucified* (1 Cor 2:2). Our salvation is in this, and only in this!

CHAPTER 2

The Importance
of Spiritual Discernment

*But the natural man does not receive the things of the Spirit
of God: for they are foolishness to him: nor can he know them,
because they are spiritually discerned.* (1 Cor 2:14)

Why is the above quote true? Why does the "natural"
man not accept that which is from the Spirit of God?
And more so, how can he consider it "foolishness"? What
does it mean to discern spiritually?

Generally speaking, that person who exhibits the best personality traits—a person who is good and warm-hearted—
is usually called an "affable, soulful man." Why then cannot
such a person understand that which is from the "Spirit of
God," even consider it "foolishness"? Were we not taught
even in childhood that a person consists of soul and body?
That even though the body was made of the earth, the soul
is a higher principle, of divine origin, and strives towards
God. How then can this soul not know the Spirit of God
and not accept that which comes from the Spirit? Here, the
Apostle Jude the Brother of the Lord, in his General Epistle
writes that, *These are sensual persons, who cause divisions, not*

having the Spirit (Jude 1:19). Who are these sensual people? Why does the Word of God speak of them disapprovingly?

The concept that a person consists of body and soul is too elementary, primitive; in fact, a person's makeup is more complex. When one says that we consist of body and soul, one wants to express the fact that a person is made up not only of inert material but also of a higher principle, which enlivens the material, makes it come alive. *Man became a living being* (Gen 2:7), and after God made man from the earth, He *breathed into his nostrils the breath of life* (Gen 2:7). In this manner, every living thing has a soul, every animal:

> *Then God said, "Let the waters abound with an abundance of living creatures"* . . . *So God created great sea creatures and every living thing* [animal soul] *that moves, with which the waters abounded, according to their kind, and every winged bird according to its kind. And God saw that it was good* . . . *Then God said, "Let the earth bring forth the living creature* [living soul] *according to its kind: cattle and creeping thing and beast of the earth, each according to its kind: and it was so.* (Gen 1:20–24)

Thus, in essence, the soul is to be known only as the life source in every living thing, and nothing more.

In this respect, the Lord's statement, *For whoever desires to save his life* [soul] *will lose it, but whoever loses his life* [soul] *for My sake and the gospel's will save it* (Mark 8:35), becomes entirely clear.

Without an explanation, the Lord's words may seem to many people incomprehensible, even scandalous. The "soul" in the above excerpt is to be understood as the life force, as that which gives life to an otherwise dead body, and nothing more. Thus, the text above takes on an entirely different meaning. The person who wants to save his life [soul]—that is, he who holds on too dearly to his earthly life—will lose it, but the person who gives up his life [soul] for Christ and the Gospel will be the only one who gains true life, not this temporary life but the future, eternal one. Therefore, the understanding that a person consists of body and soul is a primitive one, far from the deep concept of the complexity of human nature. In St Paul's Epistle to the Hebrews, we find a more detailed understanding of the makeup of a human. St Paul says, *For the word of God is living and powerful, and sharper than any two-edged sword, piercing even to the division of soul and spirit, and of joints and marrow, and is a discerner of the thoughts and intents of the heart* (Heb 4:12).

Here, we can see how "soul" is differentiated from "spirit." This differentiation between "spiritual" and "worldly" is found in many places in Sacred Scripture. Therefore, the Church has determined that a person's nature has a triple makeup, consisting of a body, a soul, and a spirit, with the highest being the spirit. The soul, although higher than the body, because it is immaterial and without substance, is, according to St Theophan the Recluse, the great psychologist and master of the spiritual life, "entirely directed towards the ordering of our temporal existence, our earthly one . . . the soul's knowledge is built only on the basis of that which is gained through experience from life around us. The activity of the soul is directed towards the fulfillment of the demands of temporal life."[1] Therefore, the soul is a lower principle compared to the spirit in a person and is closely connected to the body and to the life of the body.

At the same time, the soul acts as a bond between the body and the spirit, functioning like a bridge from the body to the spirit.

As we see, a person is tripartite. How does each part function in our nature?

God created the body *of the dust of the ground* (Gen 2:7) and thus the body belongs to the earth. It was said to the first human, *For dust you are, and to dust you shall return.* (Gen. 3:19). The life of the body consists of satisfying the needs of the body. In the life of his body, a human does not in any way differ from other living animals. The needs of the body are multifaceted, depending on the various organs, but generally these needs center on the fulfilling of two basic instincts—the instinct of self-preservation and the instinct to reproduce. Both of these instincts have been placed by the Creator into the corporeal nature of all living things with a fully understandable purpose, in order that living creatures should not perish and become extinct. To have a relationship with the external world, the body of a person is endowed with five senses—vision, hearing, touch, taste, and smell—without which a person would be totally help-less in the world. The entire apparatus of the human body is astoundingly complex and wisely fashioned. Alone, without a life-giving soul, the body would be a lifeless machine.

The soul is given by God as the life-giving force of the body in order for the body to function. All actions and all movements of the soul are so diversified, so complex, so intertwined with each other, so mutable, and frequently difficult to discern, that it is common to separate them into three categories for convenience: thoughts, feelings, and desires. These movements of the soul are the study of a specific science called psychology. Psychology, in conjunction with the three categories of the soul's activity, is divided into three areas: (1) the psychology of *cognition*, (2) the psychology of *feelings*, and (3) the psychology of *the will*. The area of cognition refers to imagination and memory, which use the mind to gather knowledge and understanding. Understanding and knowledge, organized by mental labor into an orderly fashion or system, give us the sciences. The brain is the organ of the body that the soul uses for mental labor.

The organ of feeling is usually referred to as the human heart. This is because all emotions—joy or grief, sorrow or pleasure, likes or dislikes, anger or a peaceful disposition of spirit, calm or agitation—always resound in the heart, either by adding energy or slowing down its activity. The heart registers what is pleasant or unpleasant. Because a person naturally strives towards that which is pleasant and desires to avoid that which is distasteful, the heart becomes the center of our life, the place where all that enters from the outside is contained and out of which comes all that is within.

The will controls a person's desires and is not centered in any organ. The will acts out throughout the parts of the body, and those parts set our body in motion through a decision of the will on to the muscles and nerves.

The result of the activity of our mind and feelings, given birth by the heart, has an effect on the will, which results in bodily movement or action. Thus, the soul and body are intricately connected. The body, by means of the sensory organs, conveys impressions to the soul; and the soul, depending on the impressions, will direct the body in a corresponding manner, controlling its activity. The close connection between the soul and body is frequently referred to by the term "psychosomatic." Still, we must differentiate between the life of the body as a means of fulfilling the needs of the body and the life of the soul as satisfying the needs of the soul. We already know what the life of the body consists of: self-preservation and perpetuation of the species. The life of the soul consists of satisfying the needs of the mind, feelings, and the will. The soul wants to acquire knowledge and experience a variety of feelings.

Mere existence does not fully satisfy all the needs of the soul and body. The body and soul are not the complete, whole person. Something higher stands above the body and soul, frequently playing the role of judge of soul and body, evaluating it from a unique, elevated perspective. This higher principle in a person is the spirit, and its origin is divine. This is the power which God breathed into the face of man, having completed His creation. Animals have a soul, but the soul, according to Genesis (1:24), together with the body, was made from the earth. The human soul is in many ways similar to that of the animals, but our soul's higher part is incomparably superior to that of the animals. This superiority depends on the communion of the soul with the spirit, which is from God.

What is this spirit and how does it reveal itself?

In his book *The Spiritual Life and How to Be Attuned to It,* Bishop Theophan the Recluse wrote:

The spirit as a force proceeding from God, knows God, seeks after God and only in Him finds its rest. By means of some kind of hidden spiritual sensitivity, the spirit is convinced of its origin in God. The spirit feels its total dependency on Him and acknowledges that it is obliged to please God in every way and live in Him and for Him.

St Augustine wrote, "Thou O Lord, hast created us with a striving for Thee, and our heart is not at rest until it rests in Thee."

1. How does the spirit reveal itself in a person? St Theophan indicates three manifestations of the Spirit: (1) the fear of God, (2) the conscience, and (3) the thirst for God: "All people, no matter what degree of development they have reached, know that there is a Supreme Being, God, Who created everything, maintains everything and rules everything, and that they depend on Him in everything, that they must please Him, that He is the Judge and Requiter, Who gives to everyone according to his deeds. Such is the natural credo which is inscribed in the spirit. By confessing it the spirit venerates God and is filled with the fear of God."

2. Acknowledging itself to be obliged to please God, the soul would not know how to satisfy this obligation if the conscience did not rule it in this area. "[The conscience] indicates what is right and wrong, what is pleasing to God and what is displeasing, what should be done and what should not be done." However, the conscience does not only dictate but compels the person to do what he should as well as "rewarding compliance with comfort and punishing

noncompliance with remorse. The conscience is the legislator, the guardian of the law, the judge, and the executor." It is no coincidence that the people call the conscience "the voice of God."

3.   It is the property of the spirit to seek God, to strive towards Him, to thirst for Him. Nothing created, earthly, worldly can ever satisfy it. No matter how many good things a person has, it will never seem enough, he will always want more and more. This eternal lack of fulfillment, this constant dissatisfaction proves that our spirit strives towards something Higher, the Ideal, as they say. Therefore, nothing earthly can replace this Higher Being, this Ideal. The soul is restless, finding no peace. Only in God, in living communion with Him, can a person find total satisfaction and rest, having obtained grace-filled peace of soul and calmness.

These are the manifestations of the spirit in a person. Now it should be clear what the spiritual life consists of, in contrast to the life of the soul and body. The spiritual life consists of satisfying the needs of the spirit, and the needs of the spirit consist of a person's striving towards God, seeking for living communion with Him, and the desire to live according to God's will.

Is this the way people today understand the spiritual life? Our times are characterized by all kinds of masquerading, falsity, manipulation, perversity, and malicious distortions. This is quite understandable. The flaunting spirit of self-validating pride is clearly unattractive, just as is its father, Satan. Therefore, this evil spirit of pride must masquerade, hide itself behind various seemingly well-intended disguises. It is no accident that, according to St Paul, Satan transforms himself into *an angel of light*. The modern view of things is perverted and distorted to the point of being unrecognizable.

This is how the matter now stands considering the spiritual life. A person's spirit is completely ignored by our contemporaries. They combine the spirit and the soul into one. Moreover, in contemporary psychology, the manifestations of the spirit are perceived to be part of the life of the soul—religious feeling, moral feeling, and the conscience are considered part of the soul's functions. Materialists reject the soul completely and consider its functions as part of the brain and nervous system. Consequently, they deem spiritual life to be materialistic manifestations, examining them as brain functions, the nervous system, etc. Here, we have the crudest and most primitive profanation of what we understand to be spiritual life. Modern man frequently does not differentiate between the actions of the body, the soul, and the spiritual life, thus mixing them up, creating total confusion. It comes as no surprise now when we hear the expression "spiritual life," which can mean absolutely anything except that which is authentic spiritual life. Science, and all types of discoveries and inventions—cinema, theater, ballet, and even the circus—are lumped together into the area of spirituality. In other words, what is emotional or natural is assumed to be spiritual and that which relates exclusively to the secular is misunderstood to be "spiritual life."

Why has this falsification taken place? Why has spiritual life become the inheritance of a few chosen individuals?

This has happened because the self-confirming spirit of human pride has become the dominant spirit of our times. Authentic spiritual life—the striving of the human spirit towards God—naturally assumes a living faith in a personal God and a sincere desire to live according to the dictates of the conscience, all of which are absent in the majority of modern people. As we have already noted, the spirit of self-asserting human pride strives to establish faith in itself in place of faith in God. The voice of the conscience unmasks this deception and, in general, deters the freedom to act in such a way and is suppressed and extinguished by pride. The existence of the spirit is rejected and ignored, and the first place is given to the soul, that is, the rule of the mind, feelings, and will. The soul, although lower than the spirit, occupies the main place in human life. That is why the Word of God calls such a person "worldly," maintaining that what is spiritual is incomprehensible and foreign to him, and therefore he cannot understand or accept what proceeds from the Spirit of God.

However, no matter how much a person suppresses within himself the needs of the spirit, these needs will demand their rights. The spirit yearns for God and, unable to find a means of escape for its aspirations under the violent pressure of the crude oppression of human pride, the spirit satisfies itself by substitutes, which are invented by the same human pride in order to calm it. In place of authentic religion, the spirit is given some nebulous philosophical teaching, or theosophy, or spiritism. In place of the Church, it is offered the "temple" of science, or the theater, ballet, etc.—anything from worldly life, capable of fully captivating the person. This kind of forgery, the substitute for spirituality by something emotional, is a defining characteristic of our times.

For example, many of us from Russia, in the past and at present, have gone to church only for some aesthetic feeling, to listen to beautiful singing. There is no arguing that aesthetic feeling is of course an exalted sensation, a sense for the beautiful in the soul, a reflection of a higher Divine Beauty. However, to the degree that it remains unconscious, detached from any awareness of attraction towards God, it still remains in the realm of worldliness and is foreign to genuine spirituality.

In their highest manifestation worldly, earthly feelings are so close to spiritual ones that it is difficult for modern man to differentiate between them. He takes the "emotional" to mean "spiritual." Sometimes it seems to him that he receives total "spiritual satisfaction" from what is earthly; however, he is only deceiving himself, he is deluded. One person who was very intellectually and culturally developed admitted to me that when he listened to music he had an experience of prayer. How, in fact, can we tell the difference between a natural state and a genuine spiritual one? A genuine spiritual state is always totally passionless, so exalted that it lifts a person above the earth, not offering him any worldly sensations. On the other hand, every natural, worldly state, no matter how elevated it may be, will, without fail, stimulate some worldly, carnal sensation—for example, rapid heartbeat, pleasurable scintillation of the nerves, goose bumps—which frequently appear when people listen to beautiful music or singing. This overwhelming dominance of emotionalism in contemporary people explains why genuine, strict church singing, which satisfies only spirituality, is bewildering and boring for the majority, even for those considered to be churchgoing. They do not like it. We have replaced strict church singing of the past two centuries with Italian, concert singing, which satisfies the worldly-minded and is, therefore, favored by our contemporaries who wallow in emotionalism. Likewise, modern people do not like ancient iconography because their spiritual sensitivity is not developed enough to understand and value the spiritual beauty of the sacred images of antiquity that renounce this world. A worldly-minded person is more attracted to full-faced, rosy-cheeked Madonnas, who remind him of this world rather than the exalted spiritual world. Likewise, as in other issues related to genuine spiritually, modern man is dim-witted and deaf, while at the same very sensitive to worldly things that he often takes to be "spiritual," even officially calling them so in the press, literature, and public forums.

Why is spiritual life so suppressed in our times and why has worldly thinking taken over? We have already mentioned that this occurs because the spirit of modernity, the spirit of self-proclaimed pride has made it a goal to exterminate the idea of God from the lives of people now and to deify man as the god for modern times.

The whole lifestyle of modern man is arranged in such a way that there is no place for genuine spiritual life. Those who seek the spiritual life are thrown into despair, driven further and further into the mire of worldliness. The very pulse of modern life is nervous, refusing to allow a person any solitude for self-examination, creating an atmosphere hostile to leading a spiritual life. Modern man is like a screw or cogwheel in the gigantic machine of materialistic culture. He loses his individuality and personality and, as they say, runs in circles like a hamster in his cage. "Time is money" is the catchword for modern man's lifestyle, therefore allowing no time for self-reflection, introspection, attention to the movements of one's spirit and to the voice of one's conscience. This nervous, rabid lifestyle wears one out entirely, drains a person's energy and, thus, leaves him no time to work on himself, which is a necessary demand of the spiritual life. The only desire that remains is to be entertained, to relax, and to get away for a time from the oppressive mechanism of life. As a result, now all kinds of cheap, light-minded entertainment abound—movies, discotheques, etc., and places to spend free time from work and study. Without a doubt, this is the curse of modern life, corrupting all that is healthy in a person. It is the inevitable offspring of modern culture, of a person who has renounced God and made the foundation of his life the spirit of self-satisfying human pride.

All of modern entertainment acts like cocaine and alcohol on our contemporaries. Contemporary entertainment puts spiritual life to sleep in man, paralyzes spiritual impulses, and suppresses the voice of the conscience and of moral norms. Little by little, a person descends from the natural to gross carnality, becoming like a body without a soul according to the words of the Psalmist, *I was so foolish and ignorant: I was like a beast before you* (Ps 73:22). The terrible sentence of God, once directed to the contemporaries of righteous Noah who perished in the flood, is pronounced on such people: *And the Lord said, "My spirit shall not always strive with man forever, for that he also is indeed flesh . . ."* (Gen 6:3).

When a person created in the image and likeness of God renounces his high calling and becomes a soulless body, he *becomes like a brute beast* and pronounces upon himself his own death sentence. The latest events in history are the best proof of just how destructive for man it is to forget about spiritual life, to replace it by worldly thinking, and then descend into total depravity.

Forgetting God and then declaring the divinity of man leads people further and further into moral decay, leading to animal-like behavior and self-destruction. Therefore, it is as clear as day that the only salvation for mankind out of complete ruin is spiritual life, although not that "spiritual life" offered to moderns by their cultural guides who falsify and replace "spirituality" with "worldly thinking," but genuine spiritual life, which manifests itself in striving towards God, in searching to commune with Him and in the desire to live by His Holy Will.

CHAPTER 3

Gospel Love and Humanistic Altruism

God is love, and he who abides in love abides in God, and God in Him. (1 John 4:16)

The spirit of self-asserting human pride has brought with it division, wickedness, and hate into our world. In ancient Rome, this shared wickedness and hatred among people gave birth to the saying, "Man is a wolf to man." It is impossible to build a life based on wickedness and hatred, for they are principles of destruction. Therefore, the Incarnate Only-Begotten Son of God, our Lord Jesus Christ, brought to earth a new commandment, a new law, the law of love. *A new commandment I give to you,* the Lord said to His Holy Apostles at the Mystical Supper, *That you love one another, as I have loved you, that you also love one another. By this all will know that you are My disciples, if you have love for one another* (John 13:34–35). This mutual love is a distinguishing characteristic of Christianity. Therefore, where there is no love, there is no Christianity.

Why is this so? Because love is the only creative force in life; it is the source, the root, the well-spring of all creation.

The only reason for the creation of the world and man by God the Creator is His love. God's love can never stand alone; it always seeks an object upon which it can pour itself out, make it joyful and prosperous. Divine love created the world; divine love continues ceaselessly to care and providentially provide for man after the fall, despite man's lack of fidelity to God. Divine love raised the Only-Begotten Son of God upon the Cross in order to deliver man from the torments of hell, which man deserved. This same love, having called forth a response of fiery love in the souls of the first Christians, inspired them to endure terrible tortures for Christ's name. This same love, burning in the hearts of ascetic strugglers, inspired them to renounce the sinful world, impelled them to mortify the flesh and subjugate it, making it easier to be united with Christ. This love ennobles our entire life; it creates and inspires all that is truly great, truly beautiful. Family life, society, and government are grounded in this love. In short, love is the vivifying, fundamental life-giver of the world. This is fully logical, for love is from God, and God Himself is love.

The entire essence of the law of the Gospel lies in the teaching about love, brought down by the Incarnate Son of God. When a certain lawyer of the Old Testament Law approached Jesus Christ, tempting Him and saying, "What is the greatest commandment of the law?" the Gospel says Jesus answered: *You shall love the Lord your God with all your heart, with all your soul, and with all your mind. This is the first and great commandment. And the second is like it: "You shall love your neighbor as yourself." On these two commandments hang all the Law and the Prophets* (Matt 22:37–40). Love is the foundation of the entire law of the Gospel: in the first place love for God, in the second, love for our neighbor. Contained in these two commandments is the entire Gospel; thus, they are referred to as the "Short Gospel."

Yet note what happens next. Having given the commandments of love for God and neighbor, our Lord Jesus Christ immediately adds His teaching about His Sonship to the Father and about His divinity:

> *When the Pharisees were gathered together, Jesus asked them, saying, "What do you think about the Christ? Whose Son is He? They said to him, "The Son of David." He said to them, "How then does David in the Spirit call him 'Lord,' saying, 'The Lord said to my Lord, 'Sit at My right hand, Till I make Your enemies Your footstool?' If David then call Him 'Lord,' how is He his Son?" And no one was able to answer Him a word, nor from that day on did anyone dare question Him anymore.* (Matt 22:41–46)

What does this signify? What is the connection between the teaching of love and the teaching about the divinity of our Lord Jesus Christ? Nothing happens by accident. Even more so, nothing just as a turn of speech, so to say, in the very words of the Lord Jesus Christ. There, everything always breathes an unearthly wisdom and endless depth of logical thought and significance. In His commandment on love as the basis of the law of the Gospel, the Lord connected it to the teaching about Himself as the Son of God. Without faith in Jesus Christ as the Son of God, there cannot be true love for God or for neighbor. True, unselfish, pure love for God and man is impossible except under the action of faith in the divinity of

Christ the Saviour—faith in the fact that He is the Incarnate Son of God who came down to earth to save mankind.

Why is this so? Because only that kind of faith in the Son of God—an ardent, living, burning faith in the One who humbled Himself for our sake and gave Himself up to a disgraceful, tortuous death for us—is capable of igniting within us a grateful response of love towards God. This love inspires us with a burning desire to live according to His holy will, never to offend Him, and consequently to love our neighbors as fellow children of God, as our brothers in Christ for whom Christ our Saviour also spilled out His most pure blood.

Besides all this, our nature is so broken by sin, that without such faith in the salvific Grace of God given to us by the Son of God's sufferings on the Cross, without this grace-filled sanctification and illumination, we are incapable of doing anything truly good; we are incapable of pure, unselfish love for God and neighbor. Without sanctification and illumination from above, our love—if it indeed is within us—lacks Gospel purity and holiness. It is poisoned by our self-love and egoism, which is so subtle and hard to grasp that we do not even notice it. We think that we truly love God and our neighbor, but in reality this is self-love, not love for God and neighbor. A person thus deceives both himself and his neighbor. Only the all-powerful Grace of God, which heals sinful depravity and refashions man, mortifying the egotistical principle of self-love—only that Grace is capable of kindling a spark of true, pure, selfless love.

The spirit of modernity or, otherwise put, the spirit of self-asserting human pride, although incapable of totally denying love as a creative force in man, nonetheless attempts to distort that healthful Gospel teaching on love, substituting it with its own type of love, where self-love strives to establish itself even more. Since the time of the Renaissance, the Gospel's teaching on love has been supplanted by the concepts of "altruism," "philanthropy," and so-called situational ethics, a morality independent of religion, of faith in God, and of the law of God. The advocates of this irreligious morality attempt to convince everyone that "one can be a true Christian without believing in Christ." In other words, one can be a nonbeliever, not religious, and at the same time do good to one's neighbor and lead a blameless, morally praiseworthy life. These kinds of do-gooders are called "altruists" or "philanthropists." They say that faith in God is unnecessary, that only people of primitive cultural development need such faith as a constraining element to reign in their otherwise uncontrollable egotistical instincts. There exist proponents of "altruism" who even try to prove that religious—and specifically, Christian—morality is inferior to autonomous morality. According to their understanding about life, they claim that the religious person, and particularly the Christian, does good through mercenary and selfish motives, in order to obtain a reward in the future life and avoid the torments of hell. On the other hand, the nonreligious, altruist-philanthropist apparently does good for goodness' sake. Therefore, they claim that the motivation in nonreligious morality is superior to that in Christian morality! Finally, they say that although there are some very religious people who pray long and hard to God, such people are egotists, cruel and heartless; they not only fail to do good deeds for others, but even strive to exploit others for their own personal gain. These critics conclude that religiosity does not save one from egoism. Therefore, according to them, it is not logical to look for a close connection between religion and morality, as the Gospel preachers contend.

Is the above really true? We must examine all of these assumptions in order to understand their fallacies.

First, it is impossible to call a person a "Christian," even more so a true Christian, who does not believe in Christ, even if he does good for others. Christianity does not consist of merely doing good. It is not just about morality. A Christian is one who totally accepts the teaching of our Lord Jesus Christ. The Christian adopts this teaching completely as his all-encompassing worldview. Jesus Christ taught not only about doing good to your neighbor, but about faith in God and in Himself as the Incarnate Son of God, making this faith the necessary condition for salvation. Without faith in Jesus Christ as the Son of God, there is no Christianity. Performing good deeds out of some unknown motivation cannot be equated with Christianity.

How can it be Christianity, when Christ Himself taught that the first and greatest commandment is love for God? This understandably includes faith in Him, for how can we love someone whose existence we deny? Without love for God and faith in Him, no really authentic good deeds are possible, nor is any true morality possible. From the time of the Fall of our ancestors, who dreamed of becoming gods, egoism became so firmly embedded in human nature that the ability to do good for goodness' sake was lost. In order to derive strength from doing good, to give it a higher and more noble impetus, to be inspired to do it, to persevere in it, it is imperative for a person to fully comprehend what doing good means. Christianity makes this possible. It shows that the purpose of doing good is found in our filial love for God as our loving Father and Benefactor, as well as in our love for others as our brethren in Christ. The fatherly commandment of our loving God as well as our kinship with our neighbors inspire us to this. How could anyone argue that these are not the highest incentives imaginable for doing good?! What can possibly compare with this? Can that pitiful babbling offered by humanists—the mite of some abstract doing "good for goodness' sake" which offers nothing to the heart and mind—be compared with Christianity's offering? We perceive the love of God, as St John the Theologian says, *because He laid down His life for us. And we also ought to lay down our lives for the brethren* (1 John 3:16). *If you love me, keep My commandments* (John 14:15). Here we see the highest incentive for Christian morality set forth by Christ Himself. *And this is His commandment: that we should believe on the name of his Son Jesus Christ and love one another, as He gave us commandment* (1 John 3:23), explains the Apostle.

The advocates of some sort of autonomous morality say that there are religious people, believers in God, who at the same time do not live according to the dictates of morality and do no good deeds. From the outside this might be true, but the fault lies not in religion, but with those people. Such people have assimilated religious teaching in a purely formal, superficial, external way. This is not authentic religiosity but phariseeism, which was so definitively and strictly condemned by the Saviour Christ Himself in His words of caution and warning to His followers: *Then Jesus said to them, "Take heed and beware of the leaven of the Pharisees and the Sadducees* (Matt 16:6). The Apostle James calls faith without corresponding good works a dead faith and says that people who do not live in accordance with the demands of faith have "empty piety." *If anyone among you thinks he is religious, and does not bridle his tongue but deceives his own heart, this one's religion is useless. Pure and undefiled religion before God and the Father is this: to visit orphans and widows in their trouble, and to keep oneself unspotted from the world* (Jas 1:26–27). Thus, authentic religiosity, not one which is false and external, will exclude any phariseeism and will express itself by corresponding works of love and mercy for one's neighbor.

Finally, advocates of autonomous morality attack Christian morality as if it were motivated by primitive moral principles: fear of future torments in hell and the desire for a reward in the future life. The Gospel indeed speaks of rewards that await the righteous and punishments that will befall unrepentant sinners. However, nowhere are these rewards and punishments offered as the main, exclusive motivation for a Christian. In fact, these rewards and punishments are not the motivation but the natural end result of one's lifestyle. Christ explains that the narrow and sorrowful path of life preached by Him has as its natural end eternal joy, while the broad and easy path, counter to the Gospel, culminates in eternal grief, eternal torment. These are not incentives, not external pedagogical methods to force a person to act in a certain way. They are the natural results of a chosen lifestyle, which He warns against and makes abundantly clear. It is long overdo for us to reject that absurd and even blasphemous notion that floated over to us from Catholicism that God rewards us for good deeds and punishes us for evil ones. God does not want anyone to perish but desires all people to be saved and come to knowledge of the truth. A person destroys himself, since evil deeds frequently repeated make a person evil in his nature and incapable of experiencing that light and joy, which is the natural lot of those who are good.

The only motive of Christian morality is love, love for God as our Father and Benefactor. St John the Apostle and Evangelist says, *We love Him because He first loved us.* (1 John 4:19). *And He Himself is the propitiation for our sins, and not for ours only but also for the whole world* (1 John 2:2). *Beloved, if God so loved us, we also ought to love one another* (1 John 4:10–11). *If someone says, "I love God," and hates his brother, he is a liar: for he who does not love his brother whom he has seen, how can he love God whom he has not seen* (1 John 4:20)? *And this commandment have we from Him: That he who loves God must love his brother also* (1 John 4:21). How is our love expressed for God and what is the proof of its sincerity? The Apostle explains: *For this is the love of God, that we keep His commandments. And His commandments are not burdensome* (1 John 5:3).

What could possibly be greater than such motivation? On the other hand, what kind of real incentive does autonomous morality offer us? "Good for goodness' sake"? Such an idea is very obscure. How can such a vague motivation give us the strength to overcome our inborn egoism, or compel us to do what is of no interest or profit for us? It is completely different when we speak of love. Love is a powerful force, all conquering and dominating over our instincts, even over the strongest instinct of self-preservation. Take, for example, a mother's love, which sacrifices itself for the sake of saving her children. Such a love is commonplace and comprehensible to everyone.

If there is no God and we are not all brothers, then what is the purpose of doing good for each other? Would it not be better for each of us to live for his own pleasure, to pursue his own goals and interests? It is generally acknowledged, however, that morality and philanthropy is necessary for the world, for the ennobling and good estate of society. It is said that without morality, without mutual aid and support, society could not exist. Without it a successful life for everyone individually would not be guaranteed. That is a fact. But then we see that autonomous morality is primitive, of only relative value. I do good only as much as is necessary for my own profit and success. For example, I help my neighbor, expecting that later on he will help me, when I am in need. I do no harm to anyone to avoid being harmed in return. This is the morality of a majority of people. Can anyone place a high value on such a morality? It is not difficult to judge and answer. We can see just how durable such a morality is by the fact that all contemporary moral standards in society so easily break down. And once again the age-old animalistic egotistic struggle for survival appears: "Man is a wolf to man."

Another aspect of nonreligious morality, which frequently goes unnoticed by the person himself, is vanity. Vanity appears in a more or less crude or subtle form. Good deeds are done in order to achieve glory and respect from others, or to make a good name for oneself and gain a reputation as a benefactor and helper of the needy. This feeling of vanity is often the motivation for founders and administrators of philanthropic societies, for wealthy people who share some insignificant amount of their riches for good deeds in order to pass themselves off as philanthropists. Very often vanity is the motivating force behind sentimental people, who sincerely consider themselves to be decent people, and do good, getting teary eyed over their own good heartedness. Some people think, in all seriousness, that they are doing good for good's sake when in fact they are only feeding their own vanity.

The incentive to "do good for goodness' sake" is too nebulous and abstract to move a person to sacrifice himself for another, when in fact it covers up his vanity or some other mercenary impulse while parading good deeds. Finally, it needs to be said that if a person who does good claims he is an unbeliever, it does not mean that he is a total unbeliever in the full sense of the word, a nonreligious person, and that his morality is independent of any religious basis. There are really no completely nonreligious people, foreign to any religiosity or religious emotions. If such a person does exist, he is an exception, a freak of nature—a rare one at that. The majority of people have religious feelings, although they are suppressed, they are still active, glinting like a small spark deep in the recesses of the soul. Even if these feelings are hidden, they inspire one towards moral actions, and the person does good, stimulated by these inner feelings, sometimes subconsciously, not fully recognizing the fact.

It is absurd to maintain that a person can be truly virtuous—in the Christian sense of the word—without faith in God, without love for Him. For what purpose and in whose name will he restrain his egotistic impulses? Would it not be better for him simply to live for his own pleasure, paying no attention to the needs and interests of others, taking no account of them?

The events in our sorrowful Russian homeland clearly show unstable this "independent morality" is. The religious foundations on which Russia had lived for centuries crumbled, and with them crumbled morality. Man became an animal for whom nothing was sacred. Indeed, this is a clear and living example of what Dostoevsky said, "If there is no God, everything is permissible." This happens not only when there is no fear of punishment for sin, but above all because there is no powerful stimulus towards a moral life, that is, love for God. When love for God disappears, that which is closely connected to it, and proceeds from it, love for neighbor, also disappears. Man becomes like a beast, without shame or conscience. What kind of morality can exist here? What kind of altruism or philanthropy? These are all empty words concealing callous egoism, which for vanity's sake always arrays itself in the luxurious gown of charity.

Social charity is a fashion of our times. We must say that in this social charity the heart is not connected (although to be truthful, the name of Christ is sometimes mentioned). An enormous abyss lies between our ancient Russian acts of mercy "for Christ's sake," and contemporary, cold, soulless social charity. We do not desire to go into detail about how some people make money organizing these charities; that is obvious from daily experience. Such society-organized charities are far from being unmercenary, even in the elementary sense of the word. While taking advantage of the fruits of such social assistance, people not only experience no personal warmth, but often, accepting social benefits is accompanied by a kind of moral degradation. How eternally distant all this is from the love in the Gospel! One needs only think about this a bit more deeply to realize what an abyss lies between the doing of "good for goodness' sake" and the authentic Gospel love for one's neighbor.

What can one say about the contemporary moral state of the individual who disdains the Gospel commandments? We see this clearly in the daily life surrounding us. Are there really many unmercenary, honest, decent, noble people who can truly be depended upon, who can be trusted like one's own self? What about the shameless depravity, which our pitiful youth is subjected to from an early age, aided by all kinds of entertainment, scandalous spectacles, and indecent establishments operated by adults—sometimes even by parents! All of this is a terrible scourge of our times. Solely this moral degeneracy and corruption stems from the rejection of the Gospel and the proclamation of an "independent morality," apparently needing no religious foundation. The fruits are self-evident. Who is responsible? Who is hurling mankind into this moral ruination? It is the same, self-asserting human pride which has no desire to submit itself to the Gospel commandments, does not want to bend its iron neck and brazen brow before the authority of Christ's teaching and acknowledge that the only true, salvific path for a person is that of Gospel love, first for God, then for neighbor.

According to the words of Christ the Saviour Himself, Love for God is the first and greatest commandment of the Gospel. This makes sense, for this commandment alone provides a powerful and mighty stimulus for authentic moral life. The person who loves someone sincerely strives to do everything possible that is pleasant to him and avoids doing what is displeasing. He does not grieve or, even more so, offend or insult that person. Correspondingly, if we love God we will at all costs try to fulfill His holy will, to subject our will to the demands of the divine commandments, doing this naturally, not like slaves by force or reluctantly, complaining, displeased, but joyfully, like loving children.

God is pleased above all when we are righteous, just as nothing grieves Him more then when we sin. Therefore, if we really love God, we will strive to lead a righteous life, strive not to sin. If we love someone very much, then no matter what we do, we do it as if before their eyes, in their presence. Likewise, if we truly love God, then we never for a second forget about Him, no matter where we go or what we do. We do it all as if before Him. It naturally follows that we strive to avoid anything that would compromise us in His eyes. We fear to lower ourselves in His opinion by any dishonorable, or ignoble or shameful act. Finally, if we love someone we strive to anticipate his slightest wish, and anything that he desires we accept, submitting completely, gladly, even if it is not entirely pleasant for us. For the sake of love, and trust which results from love, we are prepared to bear the unpleasant.

Thus, in loving God, we show Him total obedience in everything. We meekly, accept everything which is sent, including sorrows and trials. We do not curse our fate, become embittered, callous in heart, but rather we strive good-heartedly to fathom the meaning of the sorrow sent, correcting our moral transgressions and failings. Thus, under the fruitful influence of love for God, our positive moral character is formed, making us useful for society and for the fulfillment of the second commandment: love for our neighbor. The litmus test of true love for God is our love for our neighbor. St John the Theologian says, *If someone says, "I love God," and hates his brother, he is a liar* (1 John 4:20). This makes perfect sense. If we truly, unhypocritically love God as our Father, then we must love our neighbors as our brothers. We must love them because God commands this love throughout the Gospel, for through this we gain the right to call ourselves His followers and children. *By this, all will know that you are My disciples, if you have love for one another* (John 13:35). *Beloved, if God so loved us, we also ought to love one another* (1 John 4:11).

Here we have the only firm foundation of real morality. Naturally, if such love is true, it does not manifest itself only in words, but above all in deeds. St John the Apostle instructs, *My little children, let us not love in word or in tongue, but in deed and in truth* (1 John 3:18). *But whoever has this world's goods, and sees his brother in need, and shuts up his heart from him, how does the love of God abide in him?* (1 John 3:17).

This love is all but absent from the world today. The world is perishing from a lack of love. Instead of love, wickedness and hatred reign—at best, an icy cold and heartless indifference to the sorrows and needs of our neighbor. The world is perishing in evil and heartlessness. Only love is capable of resurrecting it. But where can we find such love if man's natural heart is darkened by passions and full of soul-less egoism? Only the Gospel of Christ offers a love power-ful enough to rejuvenate our perishing world. Therefore, you who are perishing in the wickedness of human pride, humble yourself prostrate your iron will beneath Christ's blessed yoke. Otherwise you will not find salvation!

Come, let us weep before the Lord, who has created us, weep out all the sins of our insane pride before Him. "Come let us worship and fall down before Christ: O Son of God, who rose from the dead, save us who sing unto Thee, Alleluia."

CHAPTER 4

Acquiring Gospel Love

I n a previous lecture, we talked about the world perishing from lack of love and established that Gospel love is the only force that could save our perishing world. But how does one acquire Gospel love, and why is it lacking in modern society? The answer to this question, in part, was given in our previous lecture. Now we must further elucidate this answer in more detail.

Actual Gospel love is foreign to our fallen human nature. In our fallen state, egoism, self-love, and self-assertion appear to be innate to our nature, as Bishop Theophan the Recluse states. This assertiveness of the self is the offspring of pride. How we can destroy this pride and dash against the rock its progeny—thoughts and feelings of self-esteem and egoism—that we know. We can achieve this only through the spirit of Christian humility. We must embrace Christ and learn meekness and humility from Him, as He Himself calls us to do. But, first of all, it is necessary to believe in Christ, and confess Him as the Only-Begotten Son of God Who came into the world to save mankind. And in order to believe in Christ and accept His Gospel, one must dispose one's heart to belief in God and in the spiritual world. It is this belief that modern man lacks. Thus, he has no way of obtaining Gospel love. And thus modern society lacks love altogether.

In order to acquire the Gospel love in one's heart, it is necessary to ardently and wholeheartedly come to believe in God as our Creator and Benefactor, to contemplate God's magnificent works, to envision and be profoundly amazed by God's majesty and wisdom as reflected in His creation, and by His inexpressible love towards His creation. If we become aware of how God cares for us like an all-loving Father, and even more gently, like an adoring mother, then our hearts will be filled to overflowing with ardent and reverent love for Him.

Further, if we reflect upon the fact that God is not only our Creator and Benefactor, but also our Saviour; that He did not reject fallen Man who, in return for all of God's beneficence, repaid Him with base ingratitude, but for our sake did not spare His Only-Begotten Son, delivering Him to shameful sufferings and painful death, so that He can reunite us to Himself—if we reflect upon this astonishing labor of love, we would have to be as insensitive as stones if we did not answer God's love with love.

Regrettably, our fallen state of itself is not capable of such a love. Even if this love is present in the human being, it is always tinged with egoism or pride, with something that is not purely spiritual, but rather more emotional or carnal. This is what devalues natural love. Many people who think that they love God, in reality only love their own fancies, loving only themselves, delighting in their own emotions and sensations.

"Love God as He commanded you to love Him, and not as the self-deluded daydreamers think they love Him," writes the great teacher of spirituality, Bishop Ignatius (Brianchaninov). "Do not fabricate raptures for yourself, do not excite your nerves, do not inflame yourself with a material fire, with the fire of your blood." In other words, the true love of God has to be purely spiritual, free from every carnal emotion. To attain this love, we must suppress in ourselves any manifestation of pride, as it is imperative to have a humble heart and a contrite spirit. Only one who is humble is capable of loving God in a wholly spiritual way. A proud person loves not God, but rather merely his own love for God, admiring it, delighting in his own emotional experiences and excited nerves, which are the natural result of this egotistical and sensual love. Imagining that he loves God, the proud person loves only himself and his emotional sensations, which he prizes above genuine faithfulness and devotion to God.

What then is the true criterion of an authentic and wholly spiritual love for God? It is given to us in the Gospel. God clearly said, *If you love Me, keep My commandments* (John 14:15). *He who does not love me does not keep My words* (John 14:24). Clear and simple. In reality, one who truly loves God, not merely in word but in deed, is one who struggles wholeheartedly to fulfill God's commandments, the commandments of the Holy Gospel.

"Do you wish to acquire love for God?" asks Bishop Ignatius. "Shun every deed, word, thought, and feeling forbidden by the Holy Gospel. By your enmity towards sin, which is so hateful to the all-holy God, you will show and prove your love for God. When it happens that, due to weakness, you fall into transgressions, heal them at once by repentance."

From this we conclude: in order to learn true love for God, it is necessary to read and study the Holy Gospel, which contains all of God's commandments, that is, all that God expects from us. Bishop Ignatius says precisely this: "Do you wish to acquire love for God? Assiduously learn the commandments of the Lord in the Gospel."

Obviously, it is not enough to undertake a merely formal study. It is essential to try to apply immediately what you have learned to yourself, to your life. "Strive to fulfill the Gospel in very deed; strive to turn the Gospel virtues into your own habits, into your own qualities. For a person who loves, it is natural to fulfill the will of the beloved with exactness." So that we may truly love the Lord, we have to maintain fidelity to Him. "Fidelity is the indispensable condition of love. Without this condition, love is not possible."

Is the acquisition of love for God by studying the Gospel and earnestly striving to fulfill all of its commandments attainable by contemporary man?

Contemporary people, as we already know, in most part recognize as god and master only themselves—their own mind, spirit and intellect, and sometimes even their own base feelings and carnal pleasures. The belly is their lord, as the Apostle says. Of course, for such people the Holy Gospel is a hindrance in their pursuit of pleasure. Theoretically, they even reject the very existence of God, the spiritual world, and divine revelation. I say "theoretically" because true atheists are nonexistent. Contemporary atheists are not unbelievers, but rather theomachists—God-resisters. They themselves testify to this by having declared a crusade against God, the so-called Anti-God Front.[1] It is understandable that such people refuse to entertain any thoughts of God's existence, while others intentionally arouse in themselves a hatred for Him, as someone who gets in the way of their enjoyment of life according to their baser instincts. Approaching the Holy Gospel with strict and captious criticism, and not able to totally reject its elevated moral teachings, they try in one way or another to discredit its authority and its relevance to the lives of people.

The main targets of their attacks are those extraordinary and incomprehensible manifestations of God's Divine Providence, miracles. They assert that miracles are impossible and unfeasible as they contradict the firmly established existing laws of nature.

Can miracles really be regarded as violating the laws of nature? In order to answer this question, we must first be resolutely convinced that all the laws of nature are to a certainty well known to us. Is that really so? Scientists are constantly discovering new laws of nature hitherto unknown, with every new discovery causing astonishment and, at times, completely overturning our previous conceptions of nature. What appeared yesterday to be absolutely impossible and implausible from the standpoint of science, today becomes incontrovertible fact. Let us call to mind how, not that long ago, the French Academy of Science denounced a man as insane after he declared that he would send a message from Europe to America, and receive an answer within twenty-four hours. Likewise, not long ago, scientists considered the attempt to invent a flying apparatus that would be heavier than air to be inane, while today we know that this dream (or perhaps nightmare)[2] has been realized. Have any of nature's laws been violated in the process? Not at all! Formerly known laws of nature remained inviolate; however, new laws of nature were revealed.

Likewise, miracles can be viewed not as violations of the laws of nature, but rather as the manifestations of laws of nature that are as yet not known or understood by us. Additionally, supreme among all laws of nature is the will of the One Who created nature—God's will, which governs all laws of nature according to His own discretion and in accordance with His all-Good Providence. Miracles are not "anti-natural," but rather "super-natural," because they transcend the laws of nature that are known to us. Consequently, the presence of miracles in the Gospel and in all of Scripture does not give us the right to repudiate the authenticity of God's Word, as it does for the atheists.

Some reject the Gospel from what they allege to be loftier motives. They say that the Gospel is impracticable, that its moral principles are not viable in life. And in fact, the Gospel really is unviable if we regard the contemporary way of life as natural, normal, reasonable and immutable. Yet we have seen where this allegedly normal, natural life leads. Its ultimate end is inevitable death, the self-destruction of mankind. The malignity and hatred that prevail today can be eliminated only by contraposing them with Gospel love. Yet this love—the only kind that is capable of saving the world, of breathing new life into it—is impossible if the Gospel is not made the foundation of human life.

Tertium non datur! [There is no third option.] Either life will be renewed by Gospel love or we will see the catastrophic ruin of humanity to which its ever-increasing malignity and hatred are leading it.

All reasonable people, all political and social leaders, would do well to become preachers of love according to the Gospel, and not only preachers, but confessors as well. And all those negotiations and conferences which strive to establish a system of world peace—those are empty dreams, yet it is surprising how people cannot understand this. What prevents them from understanding? That very same spirit of self-assertive human pride, the spirit of the Antichrist, which does not accept the spirit of Christ, the spirit of meekness and humility. This is the reason why we are plummeting headlong to perdition and are on the brink of the abyss, which is ready to consume us.

Let us look further into the teaching on the Gospel love. The basis of everything is pure and genuine love for God, which is proved by sincere desire and earnest effort to fulfill the commandments of the Lord. This love for God naturally generates in us feelings of love towards our neighbor. Love for our neighbor is so closely connected with love for God that Scripture considers it as a measure of our love for God. *If someone says, "I love God," and hates his brother, he is a liar*, claims the Apostle (1 John 4:20).

To love our brothers is a need that is endemic to our nature. Contemporary man does not recognize this need, because it is suppressed and suffocated by egoism. Egoism engulfs man, but grants no happiness. Every act of love towards one's neighbor brings joy, exalting the human soul and causing it to experience a sense of light, of spiritual delight. And conversely, malice and hatred darken the soul of one who gives himself up to them, oppressing and depressing him. To confirm that this is true, you only need to carefully look at your own personal life and you will be convinced. This is why Bishop Ignatius, whom we have already quoted, says so resolutely: "What can be more delightful and pleasurable than loving one's neighbor? To love is bliss; to hate is torment."

Subconsciously, contemporary man—enslaved and oppressed by egoism—also feels this. He lacks love; he is tormented and pines for it, though his external actions may not show this. Oftentimes malice and hatred develop in a person as a result of some internal dissatisfaction that burdens him. Lacking the light and fresh air of love, he suffocates in his stifling internal world, for he does not know how to deliver himself from it, how to escape from his agonizing and depressing condition. He looks around at people he knows, trying to find someone to blame, and takes his distress out on them, but succeeds only in sinking even further into the bog of hatred. He is looking for love; however, he cannot find it in his own heart, because the way towards love leads only through faith in God, yet he, in his haughtiness, rejects God.

Painfully suffering without true love, he invents for himself different substitutes for love. This is especially prevalent in our times. Instead of belief in true religion and faith in the One and True God, there are substituted various philosophical, political or economic teachings, such as faith in a particular leader, or in democracy. Instead of love for one's neighbor—comradeship within a party, the support of those who share one's political views, even to the point of self-sacrifice. These surrogates for love of God and neighbor are nothing other than obvious proof that man has an innate need for love and that he cannot exist by breathing solely the atmosphere of malice and hatred.

Yet all this, as also familial or fleshly love, is lower than true Gospel love, and is a poor imitation of it. And even though an innate desire for true Gospel love lives in our hearts, it is difficult to achieve. "Do not think, beloved brother," says Bishop Ignatius, "that the commandment to love our neighbor was that close to our fallen heart. The commandment is spiritual; our heart is commandeered by flesh and blood. The commandment is new; yet our heart is old." In other words, true Gospel love is inaccessible to us, insofar as from a spiritual condition we have descended into a sensual condition, and live not by spiritual precepts, but according to the flesh.

"Our natural love is damaged by the fall," says Bishop Ignatius. It is poisoned by egoism. One who loves his close ones—either family or friends—with a natural love, loves them to a greater or lesser degree egoistically. This love is always mixed to a certain extent with egoism: in loving someone else, one loves not so much that person, as much as his own feelings for him, thus loving in that person not the other person, but himself.

The teachings of Christ are all directed against egoism. The task of the Christian faith is to destroy all manifestations of egoism in a person, and thus to eradicate egoism itself, and in its stead to implant true spiritual Gospel love which excludes any egoism. For this reason, the Gospel does not hold in high regard love that is of the flesh and purely emotional and that flows from the feelings of the natural heart. It is to this point that Christ the Saviour says, *Do not think that I came to bring peace on earth. I did not come to bring peace but a sword. For I have come to "set a man against his father, a daughter against her mother, and a daughter-in-law against her mother-in-law" and "a man's enemies will be those of his own household"* (Matt 10:34–36).

These words for many seem difficult to understand and even questionable. The whole point is that natural-fleshly love, egoistical love, interferes with truly spiritual Gospel love. For this reason, it is necessary to downplay this lower corporal love, to regard it as having negligible worth, in order to acquire higher Gospel love. Love your neighbor with holy love, without any admixture of egoism, and purely, without any sensuality or passion.

The fact that natural love is lower in comparison with true Gospel love is corroborated by life experience. "The most fervent natural love can easily turn into aversion, and even into a bitter hatred," says Bishop Ignatius. "Natural love has even been expressed by the dagger."

Even the highest form of natural love, maternal love, if left to its own devices and not imbued with Gospel love, is of an inferior quality. Such love desires for children earthly treasures, worldly prosperity, often not thinking of any spiritual benefits. Parental love is frequently very unreasonable and causes only harm to children, when it indulges their evil inclinations and supports them in their egotistical aspirations and predispositions. "Natural love," says Bishop

Ignatius, "procures for the beloved only earthly good. It does not think of heavenly things." What is unacceptable and especially bad for spiritual life is that the natural love is always coupled with bias and unfairness towards others. One who loves with a natural love feels unwholesome partiality towards the beloved, idealizing that person, not wanting to see any shortcomings, is ready to cater to all his faults, to hurt and offend other people for his sake, and even to commit a misdeed, if it so pleases the beloved. In other words, natural love is blind, unjust, and enslaves the one who is possessed by it. It happens that a doting mother idolizes her children to the point that she begins to perceive them as in every way superior to all other children; she is ready to take away everything from other children and give it to her own. It is obvious that this love is closely connected with egoism, for that mother who is ready to offend other children for the sake of her own, loves herself in her own children.

True Gospel love towards one's neighbor is different. It is completely in and of God. Let us call to mind how the Lord answered those who came to Him to tell Him that his mother and brothers awaited Him, while he was preaching: *"Who is My mother and who are My brothers?" And He stretched out His hand toward His disciples and said, "Here are My mother and My brothers! For whoever does the will of My Father in heaven is My brother and sister and mother"* (Matt 12:47–50). In saying this, the Lord, of course, did not renounce His Mother, for whom He had great filial respect and whom he looked after with a son's concern. He merely emphasizes that the spiritual bonds of Gospel love stand higher than the bonds of natural, familial love, and that spiritual love should always be in first place.

Spiritual love knows no unjust partiality; it is reasonable and strict, wishing for the beloved not deceptive—and often harmful—earthly treasures, but true treasures, spiritual ones. Spiritual love—holy, pure, free, being completely of God—is the Holy Spirit acting in the soul. One who loves his neighbor with holy, spiritual love wishes above all else to help him in what is most important: in the salvation of his soul, in his spiritual advancement, in coming closer to God. And so the goal of each one of us who experiences feelings of love for anyone is to cleanse this love of any unwholesome passions, striving to make it truly spiritual, reasonable, and holy.

This, of course, is not possible without faith in God and love towards Him. Contemporary society lacks true Gospel love, being guided by self-assertive pride, and, opposing God, turns a deaf ear to any mention of love for Him. This disposition of contemporary society, this inclination to oppose God, is essentially the main—and possibly the only—reason why it lacks love. Meanwhile, without love, life is not possible. Love is life, while malice and hatred, which always arise when love disappears, lead to death.

This is indeed the situation with which we are faced with now. For years we felt the ominous breath of death; yet even now, though the war is over, we still feel that there is no peace in human souls; the peace of Christ is not to be found in people's hearts. Without love, there will never be peace, but only enmity pushing humanity towards self-destruction. This is why it is so sadly ridiculous to read about various world peace conferences and negotiations that aim at the establishment of enduring peace on earth. Here the prophetic words of God are in truth being fulfilled. People thoughtlessly say, *"Peace, Peace," when there is no peace* (Jer 6:14). Why is there no peace? Because, as the Prophet Jeremiah, who correctly foresaw our times, says, *Because from the least of them even to the greatest of them, Everyone is given to covetousness; And from the prophet even to the priest, Everyone deals falsely. . . . Were they ashamed when they had committed abomination? No! They were not at all ashamed; Nor did they know how to blush* (Jer 6:13, 15).

Without Christ, peace is inconceivable, for only Christ's Gospel love can give reliable and enduring peace. *Peace I leave with you, My peace I give to you: not as the world gives do I give to you*, said Christ Himself to His disciples during the Mystical Supper (John 14:27). Whoever wants to achieve true peace on earth must approach it not through world peace conferences, where everything is based on lies and dishonesty, but through the peace of Christ, through implanting Christ's Gospel love in human hearts.

CHAPTER 5

Reawakening Our Conscience

Conscience! Is this something we dare even talk about in our time? In actuality, it is only priests who allow themselves this luxury, for they are called to continually preach God's Truth. Others brave enough to speak about this risk being branded as incorrigible, naive eccentrics, if not completely out of their mind.

Indeed, who in our shameless time thinks about the conscience? Who seriously listens to its voice? Is not the very concept of conscience now considered an archaic notion? These questions can legitimately be asked if one takes a serious look at contemporary man: his personal, family, social, and political life. The vast majority of contemporary people lives and acts as if it has no conscience whatsoever. This becomes quite obvious when one compares the political life of present-day peoples with that of the recent past. The total shamelessness in the current political arena is nothing short of shocking.

True, there are those who naively cling to the belief in the moral progress of man. "You exaggerate," I have been told, "you present the current situation much more pessimistically than it really is. Our times are not so bad. Situations in the past have been much worse, and the people were no better than they are today. It is customary to criticize the present and praise the past." There is a grain of truth in such assertions. Yet because those making them consider mankind on a path of moral progress, there is no doubt that they are woefully misguided. No one will argue that there have been times in the past when moral decay, cruelty, and savagery surpassed the current condition of man. There were people in the past that ignored their conscience, acting shamelessly. Yet we are not speaking about individuals, or about exceptional events and phenomena in human history. We are speaking of the prevailing spirit and the direction of all human life in general.

Taking this wider view into account, authentic facts point to moral regression rather than progress within current society. In human hearts, evil is taking the upper hand. Evil in our time rarely manifests itself openly, in a repugnant way. As time passes, it gets better at masquerading itself in the guise of good. Often overlooked by many is the fact that those who committed crimes in the past usually understood that they were committing evil and would often repent and try to correct their wrongdoing. In contrast, the majority of our contemporaries have lost the very concept of evil. While committing evil, they do so cold-bloodedly and without emotion. They are numb to any twinge of their conscience and thus see no need for repentance. The Holy Fathers have aptly defined this characteristic attribute of the moral condition of contemporary man as "stony insensibility."

Even secular jurisprudence with its pagan roots sees a great difference between a crime committed in the heat of passion and one which was premeditated. Coldhearted, merciless and egotistical scheming with total disregard for the welfare of others—this is particularly characteristic of our times. The prophetic words of Christ concerning the last times are being fulfilled: *And because lawlessness will abound, the love of many will grow cold* (Matt 24:12). The multitude of iniquities, transgressions of God's Law leads to this "loss of love of many," for people become unfeeling, cruel and unmerciful towards one another. When faith in God is rejected, so is the concept of sin and the need for repentance, and people turn into hardhearted criminals, capable of any heinous crime for the sake of personal gain. We have seen a transition from human to beastly behavior during this war [World War II]. I have in mind the cruel bombardment of the peaceful civilian neighborhoods of Belgrade on the very day of the Great Feast of Pascha immediately after Holy Liturgy had been served in the churches. This is in direct contrast with the previous world war, when during the great feasts both warring parties stopped their military activities, exchanged greetings and even presented gifts to one another. A mere twenty years or so, and we see such "progress" in the level of human cruelty! This regression points to a complete loss of conscience. One can cite many such examples in every sphere of human activity: in family, social, and political life.

In family life, one sees the unprecedented instability of marital ties with high incidence of infidelity and divorce, coarse disrespect of children towards their parents, the rejection of the authority of elders, self-will, perversity and shameless debauchery. On the social front, there is divisiveness into parties, always accompanied with evil slander and mutual hatred, a lack of mutual understanding, and unwillingness to work together for the benefit of society. Under the guise of service to others, we find the pursuit of one's own narrow egotistical goals: deceit, blackmail, hypocrisy, and insincerity. We can characterize the internal and external politics of many contemporary nations and their rulers in the same way. Even wars in the past, despite their brutality, were fought for some noble aim and were conducted with at least a semblance of principles and restrictions of merciless cruelty. In the past, not only were written treatises adhered to with respect, but even verbal agreements on the part of government heads were honored. Now we see such pacts as mere scraps of paper, devoid of any significance. This is understandable, for the rulers do not take God and His law into account, for they generally achieve their political power through bribery and fraud, with no intent to serve the needs of their people. Those who are honest and respectable shy away from the government's helm, not wanting to engage in dishonest activity. On the other hand, the immoral ones stop at nothing to achieve their goal of power, personal comfort and monetary gain, pushing all aside and even killing those who get in their way.

"This was always the case!" someone may quip. Yes, there were similar situations in the past, when, so to speak, "someone's eyes were gouged out," but these were exceptions to the rule. Now honest and noble rulers are the exception, and rarely do they survive, for they stand in the way and are frequently eliminated by those who want to continue in their own dark dealings. Two striking examples are:

the murder of the most noble and respectable Yugoslavian King Alexander and the poisoning of the Serbian Patriarch Barnabas. Truly one needs to be blind in order not to see how unfortunate humanity is progressing in its loss of conscience. This lack of conscience is the remarkable sign of our times, or, as some may say with tongue in cheek, our timelessness.

Yet no matter how immoral contemporary mankind has become, one cannot say that its conscience has totally vanished. One can stifle it, scorn it, pretend that it is not there, but one cannot eliminate it completely. Just because a person acts as though his conscience is nonexistent, this does not make it true, for it is the voice of God within the souls of men the purpose of which is to discern between good and evil, destined to cleave to the former and avoid the latter. God's voice will not be silenced. A person may disdain it, ignore it, and treat it as insignificant, but it will continue to speak within his soul. Sooner or later, in this life, or in full measure in the next, the conscience will present itself in its full power as the harsh and merciless judge of man, the judge of all his actions, thoughts, feelings and experiences which he self-indulgently allowed himself.

Can the conscience be destroyed if it is one of the most important manifestations of the immortal human spirit? It is an inherent part of any person, regardless of his moral state. "When God created man," says Abba Dorotheos, "He implanted within him something divine, a certain design having within itself, similar to a spark, both light and warmth; a design that enlightens the mind and shows him what is good and what is evil: this is called the conscience and it is a natural law." The Holy Apostle Paul calls the conscience *the law written in their hearts*, the hearts of men (Rom 2:15). The conscience is not only a law, however. According to the profound definition of St Theophan the Recluse, "the conscience is the legislator, the guardian of the law, the judge and executor." Not only does it show what is necessary and not necessary to do, but "having shown what to do, it forcefully compels to fulfill it," and further, "rewards with consolation for the fulfillment, but punishes with remorse for nonfulfillment." We know that the soul has thoughts, feelings and desires as part of its psychic life. Man's spirit—the exalted divine spirit within him—like the soul, also has its own thoughts, feelings and desires, but on a more exalted level. In this sense St Ignatius (Brianchaninov) calls the conscience "a subtle, joyous feeling of man's spirit that distinguishes good from evil. . . . This feeling distinguishes good from evil more clearly than the mind. It is more difficult to beguile the conscience than the mind, and the conscience carries out a prolonged battle with the beguiled mind which has been fortified by the sin-loving will." In other words, no logical arguments or excuses of the mind can silence the voice of the conscience, which will continue to assert itself. If so, you may say, why have people stopped reckoning with their conscience?

There are particular reasons for this. The conscience is similar to a very sensitive and fragile instrument which needs to be handled with care. Negligent handling damages such instruments, and they are no longer able to fulfill their purpose. So it is with the conscience: it hardens and becomes insensitive from an inattentive and careless attitude. It is impossible to kill the conscience, but it can be numbed, smothered and lulled to sleep. The Holy Fathers teach us that this happens through willful sin. "Every sin," says St Ignatius (Brianchaninov), "leaves a harmful impression on the conscience. A constant willfully sinful life as it were, mortifies it."

This explains the lack of conscience in our times. Self-assertive human pride has pronounced man himself as god. All his thoughts, feelings and desires are accepted as completely natural and lawful. There is no sin. For such a man, all is lawful, all is allowable. The voice of conscience is rejected with indignation as a vestige of times past, a superstition hindering the man-god from living for pleasure. Scientific theories to explain the conscience have now appeared. How intricately the mind works in order to justify the sin-loving will! Such scientists claim that the conscience is a complex of emotional phenomena with no divine component. It is founded upon the basic instinct of self-preservation and simply dictates what a person should do to prevent harm to himself in this earthly life. For example, it suggests that he not do evil to others, for they, in turn, will not do him harm. He should do good, so others would respond likewise. In other words, the conscience is a very simple mechanism which arises from the most ordinary, egotistical motives. Like any feeling, it can be blind and mistaken. Therefore, it is not necessary to reckon with the conscience, for contemporary man is so highly civilized compared to his uncultured ancestors who relied upon it, that he can act according to his reason alone. Can we agree with this "scientific" approach? Such scientists have deadened their own consciences.

One can ask: why then does the conscience at times suggest an action which is totally contrary to the instinct of self-preservation, and even threatens one with deprivation and death? For example, a man may be compelled to share his last food with others, to give his life in order to save another's life. Let us recall with what joy the first Christians went to suffer martyrdom for the name of Christ and what deprivations the ascetics endured for His sake. Truly the source of the conscience is divine and is in no way a natural consequence of man's ego.

Because happiness in both this world and the next consists of doing God's will, the Holy Fathers, as experts in the spiritual life, beckon us to pay careful attention to our conscience. If we do so, they tell us, then it will reliably and precisely show us the clear and direct will of God. They term this the "guarding of one's conscience." Abba Dorotheos defined this as "not allowing the conscience to condemn us in any way, not to trample upon it even in the most minute of ways." The cutting edge of the conscience is very delicate. It must be carefully preserved. If a man transgresses its dictates through weakness or passion, he must shed tears of repentance." Even minor things are significant. "From those small things we also come to despise the great ones," says Abba Dorotheos. "When someone begins to say, 'What does it matter if I say that word, eat that little morsel, feast my eyes on that?' he falls into bad habits and runs the risk of gradually falling into insensibility. For both virtues and vices start from slight things and lead to greater ones, either good or bad." Man would do well to follow these wise yet simple counsels, which would have prevent the current catastrophic situation, wherein the conscience is stifled and the condition of "stony insensibility" pervades.

The only escape from such a state is to guard one's conscience. The Holy Fathers distinguish four ways of doing this: in relationship to God, to one's neighbor, to things, and to oneself. This means to fulfill all the commandments of God; to try our utmost not to hurt or harm our neighbor; to treat all material things with care, remembering that they are gifts of God, and not to be carried away with excess or luxury; and to remember one's exalted, human worth as the "image and likeness of God" and that we are obligated to present that image in purity and holiness to God Himself.

One who guards his conscience in this way will find that it will always reliably steer him into the right direction in any life circumstance. Such a man is wholesome, with a clear and certain path, characterized by calmness and equanimity, not tortured by many doubts, distractedness and cares. For him, all is clear and simple, for he has a faithful and reliable director—his conscience—that leads him straight upon the path to God Himself. Such a man has a foretaste of the blessedness of paradise within his soul; he has grasped the essence of happiness in this world, a secret unknown to many restless souls who resist the dictates of their conscience.

Terrible are the consequences of ignoring the conscience, for this leads to hardheartedness, stony insensibility, the loss of human appearance, to complete brutality. We quite graphically see this in our frightening, apocalyptic times. Man has become more terrifying than any beast. The muffled conscience will, sooner or later, awaken in each person.

Woe to those who have shamelessly trampled upon it: unspeakable hellish torments await those whose conscience has awakened too late for fruitful repentance.

The only path of salvation for contemporary man is repentance and reconciliation with the conscience in this earthly life. *Agree with your adversary quickly, while you are on the way with him, lest your adversary deliver you to the judge, the judge hand you over to the officer, and you be thrown into prison. Assuredly, I say to you, you will by no means get out of there till you have paid the last penny* (Matt 5:25–26). "Adversary" means the conscience. It is called thus because it constantly opposes our evil self-will and reminds us of what we should be doing and do not do, and chastises us for what we should not be doing, but do. This is why the Lord calls it the adversary along our way. "This path," says St Basil the Great, "is this world." Therefore, to avoid the terrible, hellish torment consisting of the hopeless agony of conscience, let us be reconciled with it in this earthly life, paying close attention to its dictates. It is the single path of salvation to which our Church calls us through the words of the Head of the Church Himself, our Lord Jesus Christ: *Repent, for the kingdom of heaven is at hand!* (Matt 4:17). As for the majority of our contemporary society who do not heed this call, who reject the Lord and those faithful to Him and His Church, we must admit that there is no hope for salvation. For evil has become second nature to them, and this is why the life of modern man paints such a dismal picture: where the conscience has been trampled, there can be nothing good.

CHAPTER 6

The Christian Understanding of Freedom

And you shall know the truth, and the truth shall make you free.
(John 8:32)

The highest gift that God bestowed upon man at his creation was the gift of freedom. Man was created free. It was within his will to choose one or another path in his life. It was within his will to obey God or not, to honor and love God as his Father, or to reject Him. It was this freedom of will that was the seal of the image and likeness of God in man. And it was this freedom of will that defined the high dignity of man—a dignity that raised him infinitely above every other creature.

Why did God create man with a free will? This is quite understandable: God's one and only motivation in creating man was His love. And love always desires the most good for its beloved. Furthermore, love desires a free response—love for love—that is in no way forced. Only this kind of love has any worth: love that flows freely from a loving heart, without any compulsion or coercion. The loving God the Father awaited just such love from the free man whom

He had created. He desired that man, whom He created and upon whom He bestowed many good things, love Him and serve Him freely, without any coercion or compulsion, as a loving son serves his beloved Father. This is the meaning of the gift of man's free will.

But, alas, man did not retain his high dignity, did not live up to the expectations of God's love, did not preserve the lofty gift of God-like freedom. He misused his freedom and fell into the most abject slavery. We know this well! The devil envied the first man, envied his blessedness in communion with the loving God the Father and resolved to wrest him away from God. This is a characteristic of all evil beings. They do not endure good people, they cannot bear those who take pleasure in good. They want to make everyone evil and, in this way, make them just as unhappy and ignorant of light and joy as they are themselves. For the devil, wallowing in the abyss of evil and deprived of the blessedness of communion with God, it was unbearably agonizing to see the blessedness of the first people. And he strove to make them just as rejected and cut off from God as he is. In this, evil beings find some kind of inner gratification, an easing of their torment.

We know that the devil was able to accomplish his goal, and he managed to do so through his principal and constant weapon: slander. Slander against God. He slandered God in front of the first people. He instilled in them a feeling of distrust in God, and with it, in place of their former love, a dislike of God, as their imagined ill-wisher.

Having created man with a free will, God gave him a negligible, easily fulfilled commandment in order to exercise and strengthen this will towards good: the commandment not to eat the fruit of the tree of the knowledge of good and evil. There could be no easier commandment. In paradise there were so many trees with wonderful fruits available to the first man, and he could delight in eating their fruit as much as he wanted. Could there have been any necessity to eat particularly from the forbidden tree? None whatsoever. However, the first man, enticed and tricked by the devil, ate. Having eaten, he immediately felt the gravity of his misdeed. His conscience instantly made him understand what great good is obedience to God, the fulfilling of His will, and what great evil is disobedience, the violation of God's will. Therefore, in the Bible, the tree that at first was called simply the "tree in the midst of the garden" began to be called the "tree of the knowledge of good and evil" after the fall into sin of the first people because it allowed the first man to know by experience what for him is good and what is evil.

Where did the transgression of God's commandment lead our ancestors?

Having refused to freely and lovingly obey God, they fell into the most bitter slavery to the devil. Before the Fall, people were completely free and moral, as though above the category of good and evil. They did not know the difference between good and evil for they did not know evil, and their souls were directed, naturally and without compulsion, towards God, the Source of all good. After the Fall, the difference between good and evil became clear to them. Nevertheless, despite the fact that its calamitous effects upon men had become apparent, evil began to attract them and to enslave their free will so much that they were nearly completely deprived of their

God-given freedom and found themselves in slavery to the source of all evil, the devil. The result for them was what the Holy Apostle Paul so eloquently describes:

> *For what I am doing, I do not understand. For what I will to do, that I do not practice; but what I hate, that I do. If, then, I do what I will not to do, I agree with the law that it is good. But now, it is no longer I who do it, but sin that dwells in me. For I know that in me (that is, in my flesh) nothing good dwells; for to will is present with me, but how to perform what is good I do not find. For the good that I will to do, I do not do; but the evil I will not to do, that I practice. Now if I do what I will not to do, it is no longer I who do it, but sin that dwells in me. I find then a law, that evil is present with me, the one who wills to do good. For I delight in the law of God according to the inward man. But I see another law in my members, warring against the law of my mind, and bringing me into captivity to the law of sin which is in my members. O wretched man that I am! Who will deliver me from this body of death?* (Rom 7:15–24)

In other words, after the Fall, sin penetrated so deeply into man's nature that, although man did not completely lose his God-given freedom and inclination towards good, he became, in the words of the Apostle, a captive to the law of sin (Rom 7:23).

Nonetheless, as a result of the corruption of man's nature by sin, his natural powers were so weakened that it became extremely difficult for him to battle evil temptations on his own. Evil grew ever stronger and established itself in man ever more firmly. Finally, it subjugated his will to such a degree that he became, in every sense of the word, a slave of evil, a slave of the devil. The devil became the true lord and master of the human race, and man's life became comparable to hell. "The devil," says St. Symeon the New Theologian, "bred spite among people and seduced them to love it. And so they arm themselves against one another, thinking that they are fulfilling their own desires but do not understand that in this way they serve the devil and are in slavery to him."

The horror of man's predicament lies in the derangement that has afflicted his mind. It seems to him that he is doing everything himself, that he is acting completely independently, but in reality he is doing only the will of his lord, the devil. "This harassing of one another," continues St Symeon, "this plunder, usurpation, and all iniquity are nothing but the consequences of this slavery. Those who have fallen into this slavery become inhuman, proud, and completely unfeeling. They do not feel any compassion towards others, nor do they perceive their own grievous condition of enslavement to the devil. Not perceiving their condition, they do not desire or seek to be delivered of it. All such people . . . because of their slavery to the devil, are parts of the devil, far removed from God and not able to be in His house for all eternity."

The Lord, who had created man out of His ineffable love, of course could not, in the words of a wonderful prayer, "for the sake of the compassion of His mercy, see man's torment by the devil."[1] "But great power was necessary," says St Symeon, "in order to free man from the hands of the devil, who had enslaved them and who was holding them captive.

And there is and can be no other power other than the One Christ the Lord, Who is the power of God the Father." Therefore, to restore to man his original, God-given freedom, the Only-Begotten Son of God descended to the earth, as though He were a slave, "taking the form of a bondservant" (Phil 2:7), in order to destroy the power and control that the devil had over the human race. By His sufferings on the Cross and glorious resurrection from the dead, He crushed the rule of the devil and then sent down upon His disciples and apostles, and through them to all believers, the grace of the Holy Spirit as the Power of God that heals all injuries from sin. He restored and strengthened man's natural powers given to him at creation, including his free will, delivering it from enslavement to the devil. From that time on, anyone who believes in the Lord Jesus Christ as the Son of God come in the flesh and who accepts His teaching in order to realize it in his life will become free again. The Lord Himself speaks of this to the Jews who believed in Him: *If you abide in My word, you are My disciples indeed. And you shall know the truth, and the truth shall make you free* (John 8:31–32).

The Jews were perplexed by these words. They did not understand that Christ the Saviour was speaking about deliverance from spiritual slavery and, thinking that He was speaking about earthly slavery, objected: *They answered Him, "We are Abraham's descendants, and have never been in bondage to anyone. How can you say, 'You will be made free'?" Jesus answered them, "Most assuredly, I say to you, whoever commits sin is a slave of sin. And a slave does not abide in the house forever, but a son abides forever. Therefore if the Son makes you free, you shall be free indeed"* (John 8:33–36).

From these words of the Lord Christ the Saviour Himself, we clearly see that the purpose of His coming to Earth consisted in nothing other than to deliver man from his slavery to sin. One who believes in the Lord Jesus Christ and conforms himself to His divine teaching becomes truly free, that is, he is delivered from the power of sin, ceases to be a slave of the devil, and becomes a child of God. "Thus," says St Symeon, "the one whom He delivers is truly free because he is pure, chaste, good, righteous, pious, loving, goodhearted, merciful, meek, compassionate, and temperate; in other words, he is as man ought to be." It follows that true freedom is the ability to live according to God's will without hindrance. One whom sin does not entice, over whom sin has no power, and who unwaveringly advances towards the ideal of moral perfection is truly free.

Experience shows that this is true. Everyone knows by experience how agonizing and painful slavery is, when someone is under the weighty yoke of another's will, not able to do what he wants but only what he is told. In just such a painful and agonizing state of involuntary slavery is every person who is given over to sin and to various passions and vices. Every passion, every even seemingly insignificant sinful predilection results at times in unbearable inner torment, creating a true hell in one's soul. The one given over to passions and vices begins to experience already here on earth the full force of the torments of hell that await the sinner in the afterlife. Let us consider, for example, such a petty passion, such a seemingly insignificant predilection as smoking. Is this not a most genuine, burdensome, and tormenting slavery? A smoker who is not able to satisfy his passion for smoking suffers bitterly, chafes in anguish. Lacking tobacco, he is ready to give up anything, to sacrifice all for a cigarette in order to free himself from this tormenting state of discontentedness. Each smoker is a true slave who has given up his God-given freedom for a "smelly hound,"[2] as our ancestors wittily called tobacco. This is why our Holy Church unconditionally disapproves of smoking, just as it disapproves of all other sinful habits and inclinations that enslave a person's will and deprive him of emotional peace and stability. On the other hand, a person not subject to any passions or vices, who is able to rein in his sinful urges, delights in a state of true inner freedom that produces peace and joy. His soul is filled with light and a blessed feeling of "sweet, heavenly peace" that is nothing other than a foretaste of that paradisiacal blessedness that awaits the righteous.

This joyful state of inner freedom from sin in no way depends upon man's external well-being nor is it in any way related to his external circumstances. A very talented author in his historical novel about early Christian times painted the following instructive picture for comparison. A proud Roman patrician, having tasted and being satiated with all of life's pleasures and, disappointed with his empty, pointless life, lying on his luxurious bed of ivory embellished with gold, sighs wearily, "Oh, how unhappy I am!" At the same time, his slave, lying on a dirty bed of straw in the basement after an exhausting day of work, joyfully, yet with tender emotion, exclaims, "Oh, how happy I am! I have come to know Christ!"

Such is the general rule of the moral life. Only that person who in Christ has freed himself from oppressive slavery to sin and has unwaveringly chosen the bright path of a pure and virtuous Christian life is happy and joyful. And all who continue to wallow in sin and who through their sins are languishing and suffering as slaves to the devil are deeply unhappy, for they cannot find moral satisfaction, which is the only thing that can give a man happiness in life.

Thus, true freedom, which grants happiness, is freedom from sin. Is this how contemporary people understand freedom, and is this the freedom they seek?

Unfortunately, no. Modern man's conception of freedom is completely different. Therefore, chasing after illusory freedom, he has fallen into the most cruel slavery that can be imagined. We have already established that self-assertive pride is the guiding force in the life of modern man. This pride has rejected God and declared that man is god unto himself. There is no sin; anything is lawful and allowable for man. Any restriction, any constraint upon his sinful will seems to him to be a violation of his freedom. He understands freedom as the right and the opportunity to do anything that he desires. No one may restrain the man-god in his freedom. "I want, I have the right," became the slogan of modern man. "In struggle you take your rights," "life is a battle," "struggle for existence"[3]—these slogans became the guiding principles of modern life. And truly life has become a battle: a fierce battle for existence, or rather for lordship, for predominance, for exclusive possession of all earthly goods. It's only natural. One says, "I want, I have the right." Another says, "I want, I have the right," and yet a third says the same, adding, "I'm no worse than they," and on and on. This results in a dreadful conflict of human wills and claims regarding the right to do something or other, or to possess the good things in life. From this comes envy, jealousy, rivalry, hatred, enmity, robbery, murder, discord, wars—in a word, all that makes man's life hell. Where does this come from?

All of this stems from an incorrect understanding of freedom. Instead of freedom *from* sin, people began to strive for freedom *to* sin. True freedom, freedom of spirit, Christian freedom came to be considered "despotism," "coercion," the oppression of the Church, while the dissipation of one's sinful will, which leads to enslavement of the spirit, was made life's ideal. True freedom was exchanged for an illusory freedom that in fact leads to true despotism, to the agonizing tyranny of sin. For nothing on earth tortures or tyrannizes man as does sin, as a sinful passion that he has carelessly allowed to enslave him. Can we really speak about the existence of free will in a passionate smoker, an alcoholic, a man given over to debauchery, to the passions of irritability, anger, pride, love of power, and covetousness? All of these are unhappy people who know no spiritual peace, nor the true, pure, holy joy of life. These people, possessed by demons, are similar to the demoniac in the Gospel who trembled when the Lord Jesus Christ approached and began to shout, *What have I to do with You, Jesus, Son of the Most High God I beg You, do not torment me!* (Luke 8:28). To such a person, Christian freedom seems to be slavery, despotism. "The fleshly man," says St John of Kronstadt, "considers attending church, prayer, fasting, abstinence, and all the instructions and demands of the Church to be slavery, and he does not know that these are requirements of his own soul." Thus is distorted and misunderstood the true essence of things by all those who are controlled by passions.

But the full extent of their affliction becomes clear if we remember what horrors the demoniac in the Gospel had come to. He wore no clothes, and did not live in a house as others do, but in the tombs. He was so terrifying to people and so violent that no one would pass by where he lived. In other words, he completely lost all semblance of humanity and began to resemble a wild animal. Of course, not all those who have given themselves over in slavery to the passions acquire such a horrible external appearance, but in their inner state, in the disposition of their soul, they differ little from the demoniac of the Gospel. They become unsociable, savage, merciless and ferocious—terrifying to others in their savage anger and rage. We do not have to look very far for examples in modern life.

Beginning with the era of humanism, man began to move away from God in his way of thinking. He then began to lose the conception of true freedom, Christian freedom, freedom of spirit. So began his pursuit of illusory freedom—freedom from anything restraining man's animal instincts—that is, to put it bluntly, a cynical yearning for licentiousness and dissipation in everything. It is in the name of this freedom, which brings a complete degradation of morals and innumerable disasters for mankind, that all revolutions were fought, when rivers of blood were shed and human brutality reached its apex.

The most terrible thing is that, as we have said, the evil of our time has cleverly disguised itself as good, and therefore, the slogans of these revolutions seemed very seductive.

In recent times, particularly enticing and fashionable have been such slogans as "freedom of conscience," "freedom of the press," "freedom of speech," "freedom of assembly," etc. To many it seemed that these freedoms are the embodiment of supreme justice.

We have now seen what the realization of these "freedoms" has brought in actuality. In place of the expected freedom and earthly paradise, cruel slavery, not only spiritual but even physical, has followed. These "freedoms" turned out to be necessary only for those who needed free rein to sow evil among people unhindered, and to set them against each other. Instead of freedom *from* evil there is freedom *for* evil. Do people need such freedom? Is there happiness in such "freedom"? Of course not! Everyone understands this clearly, yet they continue to stubbornly seek "freedom" for themselves on account of the corruption of their nature by sin. An inescapable, vicious circle results: *For the good that I will to do, I do not do; but the evil I will not to do, that I practice* (Rom 7:19).

Why does striving for imaginary "freedoms" lead to slavery? The reason is simply that we cannot give evil free rein, because when it is not restrained in any way, it easily enslaves people. This seems so clear, yet people do not seem to understand and many become avid advocates of these imaginary "freedoms." What a terrible danger, for example, there is for humanity in the seductive "freedom of speech" and "freedom of the press"! For incomparably so much more that is harmful is said and written than that which is beneficial. These harmful words serve to enslave the hearts and minds of people and subsequently cause great unhappiness and misfortune. It is unacceptable to allow a wicked person to freely sow evil with his tongue and pen, just as it is unacceptable to allow a criminal who robs and murders to be free. This, it seems, should be perfectly clear to all, but, at the same time, far from all people today understand this. They do not understand because the decisive factor in their life is the very same self-assertive pride that cannot and does not want to submit to any restraints or limits imposed upon the sinful human will, no matter how reasonable. Instead of true freedom, moral dissipation has become the characteristic sign of our time. And this moral dissipation has led to the fact that shameless, dishonest, and insolent[4] people, as the Word of God calls them (2 Tim 3:4), have begun to prevail over those who are modest and conscientious. Under the pretense of "freedom," the wicked and the strong have enslaved the good and the weak. Thus, the hypocritical advocacy of freedom, the call to defend the rights of man, in fact resulted in the destruction of any and all freedom, in the loss of the most basic human rights. And where this imaginary freedom has not yet brought about such external enslavement and spiritual oppression, there reigns complete moral dissipation, and people are suffocating in an atmosphere of hypocrisy, lies, and every crudity.

Regarding the advocates of imaginary freedom, the Holy Apostle Peter speaks eloquently, foretelling their inevitable retribution from God. He says,

The Lord knows how to deliver the godly out of temptations and to reserve the unjust under punishment for the day of judgment, and especially those who walk according to the flesh in the

lust of uncleanness and despise authority. They are presumptu-
ous, self-willed. They are not afraid to speak evil of dignitaries,
whereas angels, who are greater in power and might, do not
bring a reviling accusation against them before the Lord. But
these, like natural brute beasts made to be caught and destroyed,
speak evil of the things they do not understand, and will utterly
perish in their own corruption, and will receive the wages of
unrighteousness, as those who count it pleasure to carouse in the
daytime. They are spots and blemishes, carousing in their own
deceptions while they feast with you, having eyes full of adultery
and that cannot cease from sin, enticing unstable souls. They
have a heart trained in covetous practices, and are accursed chil-
dren. They have forsaken the right way and gone astray, follow-
ing the way of Balaam the son of Beor, who loved the wages of
unrighteousness; but he was rebuked for his iniquity: a dumb
donkey speaking with a man's voice restrained the madness of
the prophet. These are wells without water, clouds carried by
a tempest, for whom is reserved the blackness of darkness for-
ever. For when they speak great swelling words of emptiness,
they allure through the lusts of the flesh, through lewdness, the
ones who have actually escaped from those who live in error.
While they promise them liberty, they themselves are slaves of
corruption; for by whom a person is overcome, by him also he is
brought into bondage. (2 Pet 2:9–19)

This is the strict judgment of the Word of God upon the
advocates of imaginary freedom, which gives man not freedom but agonizing slavery to sin, and through sin, slavery
to the devil himself.

For us Christians, especially those who have now witnessed such unequivocally terrible fruits of these imaginary freedoms, it should be clear that the salvation, happiness and well-being of humanity lies not in dissipation nor in unrestrained passions, but in the search for true freedom—Christian freedom, which is in the deliverance of man's soul from the sin which torments it.

CHAPTER 7

Guarding the Heart Amidst the Distractions of Life

In a remarkable literary work that has come down to us under the title *The Sayings of the Holy Fathers*, we find the following instructive account. "When Abba Anthony was contemplating the judgments of God, he asked, 'Lord, how is it that some die young, while others live to extreme old age? Why are some poor and others rich? Why do wicked people prosper and why are the just in need?' He heard a voice answering him, 'Anthony, keep your attention on yourself; these things are according to the judgment of God, and it is not to your advantage to know anything about them.'"

"Keep your attention on yourself!" This is a significant exhortation that should be everyone's watchword. "Keep your attention on yourself!" That is, be attentive to your thoughts, feelings, desires and emotional states. Be attentive to all that takes place in your soul, in your heart. Do not allow your heart to become a source of evil, for Christ the Saviour Himself says, *For out of the heart proceed evil thoughts, murders, adulteries, fornications, thefts, false witness, blasphemies* (Matt 15:19).

Where do evil thoughts in the heart originate? They do not arise there of their own accord, but emanate from outside. "Stand guard over your heart and examine the thoughts that enter therein, what is their nature?" This is the precept that the holy ascetics who worked upon cleansing their hearts of sinful passions have bequeathed to us. "Stand guard over your heart," that is, keep vigilant, keep your attention on yourself; keep attentive watch over all that happens in the innermost recesses of your soul and heart, and do not allow anything foul or unclean to enter. Our hearts are soiled by harmful impressions that we receive from outside, from the world surrounding us, which, according to the Apostle, lies *under the sway of the wicked one* (1 John 5:19).

Children, as we know, have a pure heart. Then, as they grow and are increasingly exposed to the surrounding world, which lies in wickedness, their heart is increasingly soiled, losing its initial child-like purity. Children gradually cease to be children and become adults. Adults remember their childhood with great fondness and often with tender melancholy, calling it a "golden age," their "golden childhood." And truly, childhood is "golden" because this is a time of purity of heart, when the child is unaware of the filth, evil, and vulgarity that permeate the world of adults who were unable to preserve even in part the original purity of their hearts. Only purity of heart gives man true peace, joy, and happiness. Sullying of the heart brings with it emotional gloom, agony, torments, melancholy, sorrow—everything that poisons man's life and makes it difficult and intolerable. This is why Christ the Saviour said so categorically, *Unless you are converted and become as little children, you will by no means enter the kingdom of heaven* (Matt 18:3). *For the kingdom of God is not eating and drinking, but righteousness and peace and joy in the Holy Spirit* (Rom 14:17). Righteousness, peace, and joy can dwell only in a pure, child-like heart. Therefore, those who desire to partake of righteousness, peace, and joy should strive to preserve their hearts as pure as that of a little child. The only means for doing this is "attending to oneself," that is, attentively keeping watch over one's heart in order not to let in anything base or impure, anything that might soil it or infect it with any moral taint, which would cause it to become in turn a source of evil and moral contagion for others.

From what, therefore, does one need to protect his heart? One must shield it from the disorderly influx of all sorts of harmful external impressions. This is impossible, you may say. Of course, in full measure it is impossible. It is impossible be unaffected by the impressions of this world while living in it. But it is possible to limit the onslaught of harmful impressions; it is possible and necessary to struggle internally with them, striving to eradicate them from one's heart. This, after all, is the essence of the spiritual life, which is nothing other than a struggle, particularly a struggle with sin. And the ultimate source of sin in one's soul are the harmful impressions, accepted without struggle, and allowed to bring forth their lethal fruits in the soul.

Thus, the struggle with harmful impressions is most important in spiritual life. We must strive not to allow harmful impressions into the soul. And what is necessary to accomplish this? We must more often and in greater measure keep closed the "windows of the soul," as the

Holy Fathers call our sensory organs: sight, hearing, taste, smell, and touch. We need to train ourselves, to force ourselves not to look, not to listen, taste, smell or touch just anything and everything. As soon as our intellect and conscience tell us that one or another impression that we are receiving is harmful, we need to immediately, delaying not even a minute, close the corresponding "window" of our soul, that is, that particular sensory organ through which a harmful impression is entering. If we inadvertently see something bad or harmful, we need to immediately avert our eyes, even close them, in order not to see that which, having imprinted itself on our soul, will later trouble it, disturb our inner peace. If we hear some troubling words, disturbing us or provoking unkind feelings, we need to step aside from the one speaking, even cover our ears, in order not to hear that which later will trouble and worry us, perhaps even for a long time, depriving us of emotional equilibrium.

St John of Kronstadt speaks eloquently of this in his diary:

We say: "Had I not looked, I should not have been tempted; had I not heard, my heart would not have ached; had I not tasted, I should not have desired." You see how many temptations arise from our own sight, hearing, and taste. How many have suffered and still suffer because their hearts were not firm in their good inclinations, because they imprudently looked with impure eyes, because they heard with ears unaccustomed to discern between good and evil, because they greedily tasted! The senses of the sin-loving, greedy flesh, unrestrained by reason and by God's commandments, have drawn people into various worldly passions, have darkened their minds and hearts, deprived them of peace of heart, and have taken away their free will, making them the slaves of these senses. Thus you see how necessary it is to look, listen, taste, smell, and feel prudently; or, rather, how necessary it is to guard your heart so that through your outward senses, as through a window, no sin may steal in, and that the author of sin himself, the devil, may not darken and wound that heavenly fledgling, our soul, with his poisonous and deadly arrows. (*My Life in Christ*)

Thus, it is necessary to live, as much as is possible, in such a manner as to shield one's heart in every way from receiving any kind of harmful impressions through the sensory organs. It is necessary to live one's life attentively.

The opposite of an attentive live is the distracted and destructive life which most people today lead—people who are heedless of the purity of their heart and life. Both the Scriptures and the Holy Fathers caution us against a distracted life. The Lord Jesus Christ Himself, warning us against a distracted life and encouraging us to an attentive life, said, *Watch and pray, lest you enter into temptation* (Matt 26:41), *And what I say to you, I say to all: Watch* (Mark 13:37). "Sons of the world see distraction as innocent," says St Ignatius (Brianchaninov), "but the Holy Fathers see it as the beginning of all evil." One of the greatest ascetics of old, St Poemen the Great, said, "The beginning of evil is distraction."

Why is distraction so harmful? It is quite obvious: a distracted person is not capable of being vigilant in regard to himself. He is constantly preoccupied with things outside of himself. How can he observe his own heart when the main object of his attention is not his inner life but the events of the outside world? He is not concerned with reducing the influx of external impressions but, on the contrary, lives entirely for those external impressions. His inner life interests him little or not at all: his greatest interest is the external life, the life of the surrounding world, and thus he gives free rein to his senses. To see, hear, smell, feel, and taste everything is what he perceives as the meaning and purpose of his life. His soul is like an easily accessible highway. A whirlwind of impressions follow one after another as in a kaleidoscope, and he completely immerses himself in the thoughts, feelings, and desires that they generate. How can he monitor his heart and guard it from pollution by the vileness and crudity of this world, which lies in evil? There is neither time nor opportunity for this. "Like a butterfly flutters from one flower to another, so a distracted person moves from one earthly pleasure to another, from one vain care to another," says St Ignatius. "A distracted person is like a house without doors and locks: no treasure can be kept in such a house, it is open for thieves and harlots."

Our time is primarily one of distracted lives, and understandably so. For, as we have said, the self-assertive human pride that prevails today sets as its aim not the cleansing of the heart, but the accumulation of a maximum of benefit and profit for the self, all of whose desires are considered legitimate and deserving to be immediately satisfied. *The lust of the flesh, and the lust of the eyes, and the pride of life*

(1 John 2:16)—all forms of lust are taking hold of men's souls today, and contemporary man strives to satisfy them all. It is as though modern man is afraid to miss out on something, to leave unused any comforts of this earthly, fleshly life. And so he greedily seeks far and wide all that he might avail himself of for his own benefit, for his pleasure and delight. We can confidently say that the life of modern man is nothing other than a frenzied pursuit of every kind of earthly comfort and pleasure. In this sense, the epoch that we are now living in reminds us of the epoch of the Roman Empire just before the birth of Christ, when the rallying cry of the masses was "bread and circuses!" The only difference is in the fact that ordinary bread and simple, primitive entertainment will not please anyone anymore. Now, man's refined lust demands something more refined. Bread must be specially baked and served as an accompaniment to other gourmet dishes, which are prepared according to the dictates of the art of gastronomy—or rather, gluttony. Entertainment must likewise be refined and masquerade as art, while exciting the basest, animalistic desires of man's nature.

The frenzied, neurotic tempo of modern-day life makes it difficult to find calm and peace for tired, worn-out souls. It carries away everyone, making them feel as if they are merely some kind of pitiful, weak-willed cogs in the gigantic mechanism of modern life, which has lost the Christian spirit of freedom. They themselves have become soulless flesh, enslaved by sin and all kinds of passions. Truly the modern world has become nothing other than a giant sieve through which Satan in triumphant victory sifts us unfortunate ones like wheat.

And, therefore, we are all distracted to the ultimate degree. We rush about in the pursuit of some illusory, deceptive good, but that which is most important—the one thing needful, the cleansing of the heart—that we neglect because we have no strength, no desire, no energy, we have neither the time nor opportunity to concentrate and to occupy ourselves with our inner labor.

Where does this distractedness lead us? Perhaps it is not really all that harmful or dangerous? This may seem so only at first glance. In actuality, it brings an infinite amount of evil into man's life.

The distracted man has a very simplistic and superficial understanding of all things, including the most important. He is not capable of deeply penetrating into the essence of things, of rationally and circumspectly considering what takes place around him. Therefore, his personal life is quite disorganized and fraught with blunders, and he often—at times involuntarily, due to his lack of sensitivity and thoughtfulness—causes much harm and suffering to others.

"He who is distracted," says St Ignatius, "is often inconsistent: his emotions lack depth and strength and, therefore, are unstable and short-lived." It follows that a distracted person cannot in any way be depended upon: he is an unreliable, unfaithful, light-minded person. He is inclined to let down, be unfaithful to or betray even those people by whom he is considered a close friend.

St Ignatius further says, "Love for one's neighbor is foreign to the distracted man who indifferently looks upon the distress of others and easily lays upon them burdens grievous to be borne."[1] One who is inattentive to himself, of course, cannot enter into the soul, into the emotional states, of others. Therefore, his soul remains closed to others: he cannot have sympathy or understanding for the others' woes. He is not in a state to understand what someone else is able or unable to bear, and, therefore, is faultfinding and exacting in relation to others, and often demands from them that which is impossible or beyond their strength.

Finally, according to St Ignatius (Brianchaninov), "sorrows affect a distracted man intensely, precisely because he does not expect them. He expects only joys. If the sorrow is great but quickly passes, he soon forgets about it in the bustle of distraction. Long-lasting sorrow crushes him." And this is understandable, for the distracted man's mission in life is to search out only that which is pleasant; thus, all that is unpleasant is very difficult for him to endure.

What is the result of a distracted life? Where does distractedness lead the man who gives himself up to it?

"Distractedness itself," says St Ignatius, "punishes one who abandons himself to it. In time everything comes to bore him, and he, not having acquired any substantial knowledge or impressions, is given over to agonizing and boundless despair."

And this is completely understandable. The distracted man, roaming in his thoughts and feelings solely over matters of this world, and seeking only entertainment and diversions, is soon convinced that, in the end, all is extremely boring and monotonous. Naturally, this leads him to disappointment with life, and to despair. This disillusionment may be so great that people even end their lives in suicide, unable to withstand such anguish and despondency.

The greatest harm in distractedness is that it completely paralyzes a man's spiritual development. The spiritual life is thoroughly incompatible with distractedness, for the principal condition for success in the spiritual life is in strict attention to oneself, to all states of the soul. "Without successful attention to oneself," says Abba Agathon, "it is impossible to succeed in any virtue." "All the saints," St Ignatius says, "carefully avoided distractedness. They constantly, or at least as often as possible, focused upon themselves, attending to the states of their mind and heart, and directed them according to the Gospel." It is impossible to carry out the Gospel's commandments without reading and studying the Gospel attentively and thoughtfully, and without just such an attentive and thoughtful attitude to all that takes place in the depths of our soul. But attentiveness and vigilance is impossible in a distracted life. According to St Ignatius, "Sin and the devil, who operates through sin, subtly creep into the mind and heart. Man must constantly be on guard against his invisible enemies. How can he be on guard when he is given over to distraction?"

This, incidentally, is why the Church so resolutely rises up against every type of entertainment, diversion or amusement and considers them inappropriate for Christians. All of these entertainments lead man's soul out of a state of attention to itself and force it into distraction. There is no greater enemy of the spiritual life than the passion for all kinds of performances and entertainments. From this point of view, it is completely understandable why in our time, which is so hostile to God and the spirit, this morbid passion for amusement and diversion has reached such great magnitude. And all of this, for appearance's sake, goes by the name of "cultural life" and is conducted under the pretense of philanthropy: "charity evening," "charity play," "charity ball," as though there is no other way to perform charity than by buying a ticket to an entertainment that is quite often immoral and sinful. This is the aim of the enemy of the human race, the devil: to continually sift us like wheat, forcing us to constantly spin in the whirlwind of entertainments and diversions, not allowing us to collect ourselves and contemplate our inner state, our soul.

How do we battle with distraction and how do we learn "attention to oneself" in a vigilant life?

St Ignatius says, "one needs to forbid himself every idle activity." We need to allocate our time in such a way as to be constantly occupied with sensible, useful, and practical activities. Fulfilling one's duties, private and public, without excessive fuss or agitation, will never lead to a distracted life but, on the contrary, is conducive to attention to oneself and vigilance. Distractedness is fostered by idleness or frivolous activities, which are akin to idleness. Therefore, above all, it is necessary to fear and avoid idleness. Foolish jokes and idle talk are inappropriate and harmful, yet they have become popular and are valued by people who are incapable of determining the seriousness and importance of what is being said. Also harmful is daydreaming, which drives a person out of real life into a fantastic, unreal world and causes him to be distracted by thoughts and feelings that concern nonexistent things.

In a word, it is necessary to take yourself in hand, not to allow the senses to eagerly seize upon any and all manner of external impressions but rather to occupy yourself diligently, honestly, and conscientiously with your own responsibilities, private and public, without excessive bustle and fretfulness.

We must remember well that a distracted life leads to the increase of evil in the world and that only "attention to oneself" and spiritual vigilance leads to the suppression of evil and, consequently, to the well-being of all of mankind.

CHAPTER 8

Resisting Evil

You have heard that it was said, "An eye for an eye and a tooth for a tooth." But I tell you not to resist an evil person. But whoever slaps you on your right cheek, turn the other to him also. If anyone wants to sue you and take away your tunic, let him have your cloak also. And whoever compels you to go one mile, go with him two. Give to him who asks you, and from him who wants to borrow from you do not turn away. (Matt 5:38–42)

It is common to consider the fundamental thought of this part of the Sermon on the Mount to be the expression "resist not evil." From this, people come to the unexpected and hasty conclusion that Christians should not resist evil at all, that they should resign themselves to every kind of evil and be patient. Built upon this idea is the systematic, thoroughly worked-out teaching of our well-known and talented writer Count Leo Tolstoy, *On Non-Resistance to Evil*. Based upon the words of the Saviour, "But I say unto you, That ye resist not evil," Count Tolstoy maintains that any resistance to evil, any suppression of evil in human society, except by means of verbal persuasion, is contrary to the Gospel and, therefore, unacceptable in a Christian society.

Consequently, it would seem to follow that every evil person can freely do all that he wants—cheat, rob, steal, rape—and we should calmly accept this and let such a person do all that he sees fit. Some people genuinely believe that the Gospel preaches such a complete "nonresistance to evil" and, therefore, consider the Gospel to be impracticable and unfit for application in life; they reject it, and regard it as an unrealizable, even harmful, utopia, inclined to undermine order and discipline in human society. And they would be completely correct in their negative attitude towards the Gospel if it truly taught such as Count Tolstoy interprets it.

In actuality, the Gospel's teaching is not as Count Tolstoy or as advocates of the theory of "nonresistance to evil" interpret it. For a Christian, if he is truly a Christian and not a charlatan, can never indifferently and calmly observe the triumph of evil and cannot accept evil in whatever form it may appear. It is not in vain that the Church of Christ on earth is called "militant" nor every Christian called a "warrior of Christ." The struggle against evil in all its forms is the principal task of every Christian. A Christian is worthy of his name only if he, with every possible means and in every possible measure, battles with evil for the triumph of the good, for the triumph of God's one eternal truth in the world.

It is true that the primary and fundamental task of a Christian is to battle with evil in his own soul and to suppress all evil impulses and yearnings therein. However, at the same time, we should battle with evil with all possible means when it manifests itself. We Christians can never remain indifferent to evil wherever and in whatever form it appears. It is necessary only that the battle with evil be free from a personal component. This battle with evil should always be based purely on principle and not on considerations of personal profit or gain. Furthermore, our battle, a principled battle with evil, should be free from vindictiveness, from the desire to revenge ourselves upon someone disagreeable to us, or one who is our enemy. The abovementioned words of the Saviour must be understood in just this way. Without referring to the battle with evil in general, these words only warn us against vindictiveness, against striving to take revenge for ourselves for a personal offense.

A Christian is obligated to forgive personal offenses, for, as we know from the Lord's Prayer—Forgive us our trespasses as we forgive those who trespass against us—the Lord forgives our sins only under the condition that we forgive those around us. *For if you forgive men their trespasses, your heavenly Father will also forgive you. But if you do not forgive men their trespasses, neither will your Father forgive your trespasses* (Matt 6:14–15). The Lord desires to put us on guard against being carried away by a personal, mutual enmity based on personal motives. He teaches us to love one another—not only our friends, but also our enemies. To this end, it is necessary to cast aside vindictiveness and forgive one another's personal offenses.

If we learn how to forgive one another our personal offenses, then evil will disappear from the face of the earth. People who have forgiven one another their personal offenses will cease to be bearers and disseminators of evil on the earth: evil will be destroyed and a kingdom of good and mutual love will be established. However, for this purpose, every person should work individually upon themselves for the eradication of evil in their own soul. In the first place, they should eliminate/overcome the feeling of vindictiveness that is natural for our nature that is damaged by sin.

In these terms must also the above words of Christ, Ye have heard that it hath been said, An eye for an eye, and a tooth for a tooth, be understood. That is, in the Old Testament, a certain concession was made for the vindictiveness of the Jews. But in the New Testament, in the Kingdom of love, there can be no more place for vindictiveness. Therefore, it is said, *But I tell you not to resist an evil person. But whoever slaps you on your right cheek, turn the other to him also* (Matt 5:39). For on earth all of this occurs out of enmity and particularly from personal, mutual enmity, often over matters of the most trivial kind. Pride has increased and spread among people so much and has become so malignant that sometimes not only an offensive word, but even an offensive glance or a gesture that only seems offensive is enough to make people hardened, irreconcilable enemies. "How dare he say that to me?" "How did he dare to look at me like that?" "How dare he turn his back to me?" These are the most common and widespread causes in our day of personal offenses that are never forgiven and give rise to vindictive feelings and actions. From this mutual enmity, which often snowballs to unbelievable proportions, the soul of man becomes more and more possessed and darkened by demonic spite and hate, and life becomes an unbearable hell. This is the cause of all grief, misfortune, and trouble that man experiences.

How can we avoid this increase of evil? There is one measure that is offered in the Gospel: the forgiveness of personal offenses, the battle in one's soul against the feeling of vindictiveness. One who is capable of forgiving personal offenses will live calmly and peacefully, not feeling bitter against anyone and not sowing any evil, discord, or unrest. And if everyone were to live in this way, that is, willingly and easily forgiving personal offenses, then there would not be any enmity or evil in the world, nor would sin multiply. For the one who is imbued with Christian love will not begin to sin, as "to sin" means "to do evil," and true love does not even think evil. A true Christian is a bearer of "the peace of Christ" in his soul.

However, by no means is all peace pleasing to God, nor is it necessary to cherish all peace. The Holy Fathers, instructors in the spiritual life, say that there can be "glorious discord" as well as "most disastrous unanimity." We should love only good peace, one that has a good purpose that unites with God. The Teacher of Love Himself, our Lord Jesus Christ, says that not all peace is pleasing to God and that it is not necessary to value all peace: *Do not think that I came to bring peace on earth. I did not to come to bring peace but a sword* (Matt 10:34). At the same time, the Lord constantly taught his disciples peace, meekness, and humility, and in parting at the Last Supper bestowed upon them His peace saying, *Peace I leave with you, My peace I give to you* (John 14:27). This "peace of Christ" which surpasses all understanding, according to the expression of the Apostle, is a particular peace that does not have anything in common with any other human peace. This is precisely that "good peace" which, according to the expression of the fathers, "has a good purpose and connects us with God." Every other type of peace, however attractive it may seem, should be rejected as satanic seduction. Thus, according to the Holy Fathers, where explicit impiety is concerned, we should resort to fire and the sword, and not "partake of bad leaven and be added to the number of the infected." Therefore, a Christian cannot be at peace with Satan, with patent atheists, with apostates, with theomachists,[1] nor with malicious heretics. There can be no peace with persecutors of the faith and the Church, with defamers and defilers of holy things, nor with sowers of atheism and impiety.

A Christian cannot be at peace and have friendship with thieves, murderers, rapists, nor perverts. In principle, a Christian cannot live in peace and friendship with all of those people who clearly and boldly break the Law of God, harm the peace and welfare of human society, who prevent people from drawing close to God, and introduce discord and disorder into the soul. It is necessary to steadfastly remember that when the Gospel speaks of the forgiveness of sins and offenses, it has in mind personal sins and personal offenses. However, we usually understand and do everything the other way around. Self-assertive human pride forgives everything except for personal offenses. You can be both an atheist and a blasphemer and that is fine, only don't touch me. You can be a thief and murderer, just leave me alone. You can be any type of scoundrel, but if you don't do anything bad to me personally, especially if you do something pleasing to me, then you are already a good person. The opposite is also true: if the best possible person in some way, even unintentionally, wounds our pride, then there's trouble: enmity between us is unavoidable, and he immediately becomes our mortal enemy. This is how everything is distorted. Our law is such: the one who indulges our self-assertive human pride, the one who pleases our passions is good and our best friend, but the one who speaks to us even one word of reproach, even if it contains salvific truth, immediately becomes our enemy.

Therefore, all the liberals of our time, beginning with Leo Tolstoy, themselves being quite evil and prideful by nature and completely unable to forgive personal offenses, nevertheless love to speak eloquently about Christian "forgiveness of all," altogether incorrectly understanding such forgiveness. Furthermore, they attack all civil and governmental conventions and regulations that are intended to suppress evil in society and render harmless those who bring evil to their neighbors. Such people completely ignore the whole series of places in Holy Scripture where it clearly speaks of the necessity to take decisive measures for the suppression of evil that has impudently raised its head in human society. Christ Himself, the Humble Teacher of Love, took up a whip and drove out those selling in the temple and turned over the moneychangers' tables and scattered their money.

When a gentle word of persuasion has no effect, when people are so steeped in evil that they do not yield to any admonishment and continue doing evil, a Christian cannot and should not take refuge in this teaching of the forgiveness of all, sit indifferently with his arms crossed, and apathetically watch as evil abuses good, as it increases and destroys people, his close ones. To indifferently watch the ruin of a close one by one who has lost his senses and become a bearer of evil is nothing other than the breaking of the commandment of love for one's neighbor. Every type of such evil should be immediately thwarted with the most decisive measures, even including the sacrifice of oneself in an unequal struggle. The following words express particularly this idea: Greater love hath no man than this, that a man lay down his life for his friends. These are words which our Church has long applied to those Christ-loving soldiers who heroically died for the salvation of their neighbors.

And when a gentle word of admonition for the correction of an evildoer does not bring him to his senses, then decisive and strict measures must be taken for the suppression of evil. It is for this purpose that there exist in society legitimate authorities and those whose duty it is to preserve order. The Apostle Paul says,

> *Let every soul be subject to the governing authorities. For there is no authority except from God, and the authorities that exist are appointed by God. Therefore whoever resists the authority resists the ordinance of God, and those who resist will bring judgment on themselves. For rulers are not a terror to good works, but to evil. Do you want to be unafraid of the authority? Do what is good, and you will have praise from the same. For he is God's minister to you for good. But if you do evil, be afraid; for he does not bear the sword in vain; for he is God's minister, an avenger to execute wrath on him who practices evil.*
> (Rom 13:1–4)

Thus, the word of God itself blesses, in cases of need, the use of the sword by legitimate authorities for the suppression of evil. However, the authorities should remember that they are "God's ministers" and, therefore, the sword should by no means be used for personal aims but in order to defend the truth of God. The sword should be drawn only for the defense of God's truth and for the punishment of "those who do evil." From this point of view, the Church also justifies war as an extreme, unavoidable measure for the suppression of even greater evil. That war is not simply murder as forbidden in the sixth commandment is evident at least from the fact that, when soldiers came to John the Baptist to repent and receive baptism, he did not condemn them for bearing arms and serving in the military, but exhorted them to *not intimidate anyone or accuse falsely, and be content with your wages* (Luke 3:14).

Many soldiers, even those who served under a pagan king, for example, St George the Trophy-bearer, St Dimitry of Thessalonica, etc., were glorified by the holiness of their lives and were counted among the saints and those pleasing to God. What do we do when there is no other means for the suppression of great evil other than the taking up of arms? We will have to allow that which is a lesser evil in order to avert a greater evil. But to sit indifferently, passively and watch as masses of people perish is contrary to the spirit of Christian love for one's neighbor. In this case, strength of arms may save the innocent from perishing at the hands of evildoers.

One who conceals a professional thief or murderer helps him to continue doing evil. By refusing to give him over to the authorities, to render him harmless, one thereby breaks the commandment of love for one's neighbor.

In other words, Christian love should be like God's love. The Lord loves all people but He punishes and suppresses evil, sometimes with very harsh and strict measures. So should Christian love suffer evil only to such a degree that it concerns us personally and remains more or less harmless to the glory of God and for other people. In the adverse case, the duty of Christian love is not to suffer but to suppress and punish evil, which is particularly entrusted to the ruling power.

If a thief violates someone else's property, it is necessary to hand him over for lawful judgment in order that he may not further do evil. This, if you like, is even a display of love to the thief, for impunity makes evil people even more so, and they will become ever more entrenched in it, while it is possible to restrain and even correct them by resisting this evil and by punishment.

But if your brother, driven to despair by hunger and want, and forgetting all sense of shame and his conscience, stretches out his hand to your property, what should I tell you to do in this case? Doesn't your own heart tell you that this is not the time for resistance and punishment but for compassion and mercy? Doesn't your common sense tell you that this is not some common predator who needs to be restrained, but an unfortunate person who needs to be saved from starvation, an embittered person whose calloused heart needs to be softened with sympathy and love? In this case, fulfill the command of the Lord literally: if he demands your outer garment, give him your shirt also, that is, give him more than he asks of you. According to criminal law, such an offender is distinguished from criminals and his punishment is lightened.

Thus, the words of the Lord, "resist not evil," are directed exclusively against vindictiveness and the desire to avenge yourself for offenses and in no way forbids the struggle against evil in general. We not only can but should incessantly battle against evil as true soldiers of Christ. But it is necessary to remember that, in this battle, our hearts should be free from personal bias and hostile feelings towards the bearer of evil. And in battling with those who perform evil, we should always remember that we are not fighting against the people in and of themselves, but with the evil that comes from them. Therefore, feelings of mercy and compassion that are never absent from a true Christian should always direct us in this battle. "Do not confuse man, the image of God," says St John of Kronstadt, "with the evil that is in him: we should abhor the evil but love the man and pity him." Therefore, our battle with people who have become bearers of evil should have the purpose of the suppression of the evil that is performed by them and should in no way be vindictive. The right for vengeance belongs to God, Who is the One, Righteous Judge Who Knows everyone's heart. The holy Apostle, therefore, says, *Beloved, do not avenge yourselves, but rather give place to wrath: for it is written, "Vengeance is mine; I will repay," says the Lord* (Rom 12:19).

In battling with manifestations of evil in others, we should at the same time, with no less zealousness and fervency, concern ourselves with uprooting evil in our own souls. Otherwise, our struggle will be insincere and hypocritical and, therefore, without fruit, for such a struggle will not have the blessing of God. Only one who has clean hands and a pure heart, not one whose "hand is in the cookie jar," nor one whose personal interests and partialities are mixed up in the battle, can successfully fight evil. Such a battle with personal motives will not bring good to anyone—history clearly testifies to this.

We only need to consider the meaning of events taking place in order to understand this truth. Only a "good soldier of Jesus Christ" can successfully battle with evil, one who does not bind oneself to "worldly acquisitions," that is, one who does not get tangled up in any type of personal interests or obsessions, but one who thinks only of defending God's desecrated truth and of the triumph of the Gospel truth. Such a battle with evil is blessed and will undoubtedly be crowned with victory, for God Himself will conquer for those who battle.

CHAPTER 9

Waging Unseen Warfare

We have already spoken about the fact that the principal task of every true Christian is the battle against evil and that, therefore, every Christian is called a "soldier of Christ." The relationship of every true Christian to every type of evil, wherever it may appear, is a relationship of complete and unconditional irreconcilability. With evil in and of itself, that is, with the force of evil, a Christian cannot have any agreement or compromise, for evil is the sphere of Satan, the enemy of God, while the Christian is a servant of God, a child of God according to grace through Jesus Christ. A Christian is a servant of light, but evil is the sphere of darkness. *For what fellowship has righteousness with lawlessness? And what communion has light with darkness?* says the Apostle. *And what accord has Christ with Belial?* (2 Cor 6:14–15). Therefore, it is perfectly clear and natural that the principal task in the life of a Christian, the essence of the spiritual life, is a constant, never-ending battle with evil, which does not relax, even for a moment.

But with what evil should a Christian constantly do battle? Can it be that his calling consists of incessantly observing, watching for the appearance of evil in the people surrounding him and to judge, rebuke, and punish them for this evil? The majority of people act in just such a way, which is why judgment of others and mutual attacks upon one another for evil acts, or only apparently evil acts, are increasing without limit. And this is what makes contemporary life a living hell. Each person seeks out evil in other people, reproaching, attacking and berating them, not noticing the evil in their own soul. Clearly, the Apostle's warning is being fulfilled: *If you bite and devour one another, beware lest you be consumed by one another* (Gal 5:15).

What, then, should we do? And with what evil should the Christian engage in battle?

A Christian should fight every type of evil wherever it appears, but this battle with evil should, in the first place, be a battle in his own soul. The battle with evil should begin with oneself, and only then will it be correct, reasonable, and sound. One who has fought and rooted out evil in his own soul will much more easily wage a battle with evil in the souls of other people; and the less evil remains in the soul of the soldier of Christ, the more successful this battle will be. This great truth has been completely forgotten by contemporary people who have turned away from Christianity and think that they can benefit humanity by persecuting and harassing others for things that they perceive to be evil, but which may not necessarily be so, all the while themselves remaining evil in their own souls.

"A battle with evil in my own soul" is a true Christian's fundamental motto, and it is the one true principle, the one sound and reliable foundation on which one can build the well-being of humanity. Neither mutual persecution or oppression for different political convictions, nor the brutal annihilation of dissenting individuals with which modern leaders are occupied, but the destruction of evil in one's own soul is that which is necessary. This is the only way to avoid the terrible abyss of destruction into which humanity is on the verge of careening.

All the ancient ascetics undertook this constant, never-ending, tireless battle with evil in one's own soul. They named this battle "unseen warfare" and left us priceless writings in which their wealth of experience in this battle with evil is set forth. Examples of such ascetic writings are the works of Abba Dorotheos, Saints John of the Ladder, Isaac the Syrian, Ephraim the Syrian, Macarius of Egypt, Barsanuphius the Great, John the Prophet, Theodore the Studite, Symeon the New Theologian, and many others.

The battle to which all of these holy ascetics call Christians is named "unseen warfare"—unseen by the external eyes of man, for this battle is internal and takes place inside the soul of man. In times past, the principles of this battle were also well-known to laity, to those living a secular life. This is only natural, for this battle is mandatory for all those bearing the name of Christian, without exception, as the guidelines for this battle are laid out in the Gospel, a book which is intended for all Christians.

Ever since the beginning of explicit apostasy, of the so-called age of humanism, a sharp divide between clergy and laity has developed. Laity have begun to consider themselves free to a great degree from various obligations required of them as Christians and members of the Church. They emphasize that they are "secular people" and that the fulfillment of all the rules, obligations, and traditions of the Church is not mandatory for them, but are mandatory for clergy and, especially, monastics. "We are neither monastics nor clergy," people calling themselves Christians have begun to say. "You cannot demand that from us: that is the business of monastics and priests. For us, it is not obligatory."

Thus arises a disdainful attitude towards attending church services, personal prayer, fasting, honoring feast days, the holiness of marriage, the purity of life outside of marriage, etc. Religious and moral dissipation have grown and proliferated until, finally, we have come to outright atheism and even an open battle with God and religion as something that only hinders a person and inhibits his freedom to engage in his depraved, base passions and inclinations. It is evident that there can be no question of the majority of contemporary secular people understanding the concept of unseen warfare. "Visible warfare" has taken the place of "unseen warfare" in the life of modern man. This visible warfare is a never-ending, reciprocal battle taking cover under the glib designation of "battle for survival," which supposedly is the foundation for human existence in our time. And the battle with evil being conducted by modern people is not successful for the most part because people battle not so much with evil as with other people, at the same time harboring that very same evil in their souls. Indeed, the very distinction between good and evil in contemporary humanity, fallen away from God, has become blurred: evil is often considered good, and vice versa. With such a confused understanding of good and evil, the correct and effectual battle with true evil is made more difficult.

But most importantly, we repeat, is that this basic truth is forgotten: that only one who has battled with evil in his own soul can successfully wage battle with evil in general and, therefore, the battle with evil must begin in one's own soul, with unseen warfare.

Just what is this unseen warfare? It is a continuous, inner battle that a Christian wages in order to reach Christian perfection. Inscribed in the Gospel for us Christians is an extremely high ideal towards which we can only constantly strive, without ever being able to attain it in full measure upon the earth. Therefore a vast, even limitless, field for constant movement forward, for unceasing work upon oneself, for the rooting out of evil in one's soul, and for the sowing of virtue is opened to us. This very high ideal is expressed in the words of the very Lord Himself. In teaching about the necessity for the Christian to love not only his neighbors and friends, but even his enemies, the Lord concludes His instruction with the following words: *Therefore you shall be perfect, just as your Father in heaven is perfect* (Matt 5:48).

Scripture speaks of this perfection in many places and in many ways. And what is the essence of Christian perfection? Of what does it consist? The Apostle Peter in his General Epistle explains this using the words of the Lord Himself from the Book of Leviticus: *You shall be holy, for I the Lord your God am holy* (Lev 19:2). Consequently, Christian perfection consists of holiness—that is, freedom of the soul from enslavement to sin. It stands to reason that all people without exception, not only priests or monastics, are called to this perfection or holiness that consists of freedom from sin. Christ the Saviour, Who desires that we be holy, came into the world, died, arose, ascended into the heavens, and sent down the Holy Spirit for all people, not only for priests and monastics, as contemporary secular wisdom falsely and absurdly insists. All people are called to holiness, all people are called to an unceasing battle with sin, and all people are called to unseen warfare.

This unseen warfare is not easy! It is much more difficult than any ordinary earthly warfare, for it is much easier to battle with other people than with oneself. In the words of the Holy Fathers, one who engages in this unseen warfare is fighting against himself or, more correctly, his own self-love, self-centeredness, or, in secular terminology, his egoism which is rooted in self-assertive human pride. In other words, the essence of unseen warfare is in a persistent battle with the spirit of self-assertive human pride and all its offspring—various passions and vices.

As this battle is extremely difficult, it is impossible to rely only upon one's human powers; essential also is supernatural Divine help, the power of God's grace that, as we know, is *made perfect in weakness* (2 Cor 12:9). Therefore, the Holy Fathers say that he who desires to be victorious in unseen warfare must establish the following four dispositions or inclinations in his heart: (1) never in any way rely on yourself; (2) always have in your heart complete, resolute hope in the One God; (3) work unceasingly; and (4) always be in prayer.

From this, it is clear why there can be no question of encountering unseen warfare among contemporary people who are imbued with self-assertive pride. For them, pride is more precious than anything else: it is their idol that must be served and worshipped in place of the True God. How then will they battle with pride? Presumptuousness and confidence in their own power is their principal trait. And they are not able to rely upon God because they pridefully reject Him and do not desire to know Him, much less to struggle spiritually and pray to God.

And yet, according to the teaching of the Holy Fathers, the most important and essential condition for success in unseen warfare is to "never rely on yourself in anything." Why is this so necessary? Let us examine this more in depth. From the time of the fall into sin of our ancestors, we, despite the obvious weakening of our spiritual and moral power, generally think very highly of ourselves. Although our everyday experience convinces us constantly of the falsity of such thinking, we continue to believe, in incomprehensible self-deceit, that we are "something," and even "something important." This spiritual weakness of ours, which we quite often do not notice or admit, is particularly contrary to God as it is the primary offspring of self-assertive human pride or, according to the apt expression of the Holy Fathers, "self-centeredness." It is the root, origin, and initial cause of all our passions and vices. It locks that one door in us through which the grace of God enters. This high opinion of ourselves does not allow the grace of God to enter into us and abide in us. Grace departs from such a person. For how can grace, given for enlightenment and help, enter into such a person, someone who thinks that he is something great, that he knows everything and does not need the help of others? The Lord Himself, through the prophet, speaks of such people who are imbued with a spirit of pride and vain-glory: *Woe to those who are wise in their own eyes, And prudent in their own sight* (Isa 5:21). Therefore, the Apostle admonishes us: *Do not be wise in your own opinion* (Rom 12:16).

Abhorring this evil self-conceit in us, God desires to see our sincere recognition of our own insignificance and a firm conviction that any good in us comes from Him alone as the source of all good. Desiring to instill in us this salvific disposition of spirit, God stimulates it in us either through the action of grace or through internal enlightenment, though sometimes He brings us to the recognition of our insignificance through external affliction and grief. But we ourselves should strive through our own efforts to acquire such an awareness of our nothingness.

The Holy Fathers indicate the following four dispositions for this purpose:

1. Try to perceive your weakness, basing your observations on all your life experiences, and constantly maintain an awareness of the fact that you yourself cannot do any good without God's help. St Peter Damascene says the following about this: "There is nothing greater than to realize your weakness and ignorance, and nothing worse than not to be aware of them." St Maximus the Confessor teaches that "the foundation of every virtue is the realization of human weakness." St John Chrysostom confirms, "Only one who thinks that he is nothing will know himself the best."

2. Ask God in prayer that He give you the realization of your weakness and insignificance, but first establish in yourself the conviction that you do not have this awareness and that it can be acquired only as God's gift.

3. Always fear for yourself and be wary of the crafty designs of Satan, with whom it is impossible to grapple without God's help.

4. If you happen to fall into some kind of sin, immediately recognize your weakness and complete helplessness. Impress upon yourself that God allowed this fall so that you would know better your feebleness and insignificance before God and would learn to disdain yourself.

Thus, that which is most necessary for success in unseen warfare is the recognition of one's own weakness and complete insignificance without the help of God. This awareness is so necessary that God providentially brings prideful and self-reliant people to such a recognition through falls, allowing them to lapse into one or another sin, and especially into those sins from which they considered themselves strong enough to protect themselves. "Know," says St Isaac the Syrian, "that where there was a fall, before there had lived pride." Therefore, it is essential for him who has fallen into some kind of sin to turn as quickly as possible in thought and feeling to the consciousness of his own insignificance, to reproach and humble himself in his thoughts, and to ask God to instill in him the constant awareness of his own nothingness.

In the same way, when someone is stricken with poverty, misfortune, sorrow, or sickness, it should be looked upon as a means sent by God for the recognition of one's insignificance. We must be humbled and recognize our weakness.

One who wants to thoroughly comprehend his weakness must attentively, with fervor, observe himself, his thoughts, his feelings, his words, and his actions for at least several days. One who does this will inevitably notice how sinful, foolish, and incorrect his deeds, words, feelings, and thoughts are. Then he will clearly see his own state of disarray, how inconstant he is in doing good, how insignificant he is and, therefore, that it is absurd and foolish for him to rely upon himself and to think that he is capable of performing something truly good.

You ask, "How can this be? Is it good to feel one's complete insignificance and helplessness? How can one who feels weak battle with evil in his soul?" The Holy Fathers answer that one must have the feeling of one's own powerlessness and insignificance and, at the same time, to have in one's soul complete hope in God, firm confidence in God's help. The most essential conviction that should accompany a Christian at all times is that we can rely on no one but the One God, that we cannot expect any good or help from anyone else, that only God is capable of granting us victory in the unseen warfare we are engaged in.

Such a conviction is reinforced by our belief that Almighty God can do anything He desires for us, that He, as all-knowing and wise, knows what is good and necessary for us and that He, as ever-good, is ready at any moment to help us with unspeakable love in any way that we need.

Could it really be true that the God Who gave His Only-Begotten Son to die for us, the God Who seeks sinners as the woman in the Gospel who lost a drachma, the God Who ceaselessly knocks, according to the Apocalypse, at man's heart, desiring to enter in and sup with him, that such a God would not give the man fighting with evil in his soul necessary help and all-powerful, grace-filled support? If we look into Holy Scripture, we would find countless instances of God's miraculous help for those who hope in Him. *Consider the ancient generations*, says the wise Sirach, *and see Who believed in the Lord and was put to shame?* (Sir 2:10). Such thoughts should instill in us complete hope in God Who will crown us with unquestionable victory in the unseen warfare.

But how shall we know if we are free of reliance upon ourselves and have complete hope in God?

This is known in the following way. Some may think that they do not rely upon themselves and that they place all of their hope in God. But when they fall into some sort of sin, they despair and come into a melancholy and dismal state of soul. This excessive, dismal sorrow is a sign that they hoped not in God but in themselves, and therefore this betrayal of their self-assurance through their fall is particularly difficult and torturous, and it brings them into despair. But the one who does not rely upon himself, upon his own powers, will not be particularly surprised by a fall and will not be overwhelmed with excessive sorrow; he knows and understands that this happened because of his weakness and that nothing good can be expected of him. Such a man humbly admits his weakness, his helplessness, and, therefore, instead of giving himself over to extreme sorrow, he hastens to God, pouring out in prayer before Him his repentant feelings, hastens to repent before God of his sin as soon as possible, with his whole heart, and to continue to battle with unseen enemies and with the evil living in his soul—he hastens into unseen warfare.

It is necessary to thoroughly comprehend and remember that extreme listlessness and despondency after a sin befall one as a result of pride, of excessive hope in one's own powers. When this hope is dashed, this is extremely painful for one's pride, and provokes inconsolable sorrow for which there is no place when man puts all of his hope entirely upon God and not upon his own power. Thus, excessive sadness should not be condoned, for it comes from pride and self-reliance. A humble man knows that he is weak and helpless, and that nothing good should be expected of him, and, therefore, when he sins, he does not despair but only hastens to repent.

Thus, in unseen warfare, it is first of all necessary to never in any way rely upon oneself and one's own powers, but to place all one's hope in the One God. One must struggle, constantly maintaining this frame of mind, battling with any manifestations of evil in one's self or with one's sinful passions, and to pray for the help of God's grace, without which we are powerless.

We will speak about this separately, for, as a science for battling the passions, the teaching on prayer comprises a special and vast field within the general science of the spiritual life.

CHAPTER 10

Christian Struggle

I t is in one's personal effort to eradicate evil and to implant good that the essence of Christian *struggle* or asceticism lies. One must coerce oneself in every way, constrain oneself to refrain from every type of evil, and compel oneself to every good. Unseen warfare is impossible without one's own efforts. "Water does not flow under a rock lying on the ground," as the wise Russian proverb goes. Thus it also is in the spiritual life—we cannot sit idly and wait for God to do everything for us. God very much desires to help us and truly does help us, but we receive the aid of His grace only when we apply our own efforts, our self-restraint, and self-compulsion. In this way, we show the sincerity of our striving to conquer the evil in our soul and to place good therein.

God gave man free will; He granted him the right to choose freely the path of evil or the path of good, and He does not hinder that freedom. When one is on the path of evil, God tries in various ways to bring him to his senses, to make him understand that he has chosen for himself a dangerous path. a path that will lead him to perdition. Still God does not hinder that person's freedom, but he perishes if he pays no heed to the instruction that God sends him in the form of various signs and warnings, misfortunes and troubles. If one is upon the path of good, God immediately shows His all-powerful, grace-filled support commensurate with the person's sincerity as revealed in his personal efforts.

Man's personal efforts are like a receiver for the grace of God. The greater and more decisive these efforts are, the greater is the grace-filled help from God that they attract. These efforts in and of themselves are not as significant in unseen warfare as the sincerity of one's good will that is revealed in these efforts. The more forcefully one battles, the more intense the efforts of his good will—the greater is the grace that he receives from God. Incidentally, this clearly demonstrates the significance of good deeds for salvation, an idea that is rejected by the Protestants. It is not in and of themselves that good deeds have meaning, nor is it the personal effort of doing good that saves man; what saves him is the earnestness with which his will is directed towards good. In forcing himself to do good, one shows that his will seeks virtue. This is what attracts the all-powerful grace of God which, conjoined with one's personal effort, makes him a victor over evil in his own soul, which is the ultimate purpose of unseen warfare.

The Scriptures speak many times of the necessity for these personal efforts, of the necessity for struggle. The whole of the Lord Jesus Christ's Sermon on the Mount speaks about the necessity of exerting one's efforts to direct one's will towards good, about the battle with evil feelings and inner dispositions of the soul. *Enter by the narrow gate*—thus the Lord brings to a close the Sermon on the Mount—*for wide is the gate and broad is the way that leads to destruction, and there are many who go in by it. Because narrow is the gate and difficult is the way which leads to life, and there are few who find it* (Matt 7:13–14). *Not everyone who says to Me, "Lord, Lord," shall enter the kingdom of heaven, but he who does the will of My Father in heaven* (Matt 7:21).

The Lord Jesus Christ speaks about the necessity for such personal efforts: *the kingdom of heaven suffers violence, and the violent take it by force* (Matt 11:12). The apostles, as it says in Acts, constantly taught that *we must through many tribulations enter the kingdom of God* (Acts 14:22).

From these passages of Holy Scripture, it is clear how mistaken are those who think that victory in unseen warfare and the attainment of the Kingdom of God are accomplished easily, of their own accord, only by faith in the Lord Jesus (for example, the Protestants). These scriptural quotes distinctly witness to the fact that personal labor, personal effort, or what is called struggle, are absolutely necessary for victory in unseen warfare.

True, we must not think that man is in a condition to save himself solely through his own efforts, or that these efforts are merits before God for which he receives the right to enter into the Kingdom of Heaven as a reward, as Roman Catholics think. One's personal effort in his salvation, or his personal struggle, is necessary as proof of the sincerity of his striving to conquer evil in his soul and to implant good.

This labor and effort are impossible without constant self-restraint, without constant exertion of one's will, without a persistent battle with the base, egotistical strivings of one's sinful nature. In this way, a battle arises in the soul between good strivings and bad habits. The more we exercise self-restraint, the more our bad habits weaken and the easier it becomes to overcome them.

It requires that man constantly constrain himself to do not what the sin living in his flesh desires, but that which the Law of God, the law of good, demands. Without this constant self-restraint, there can be no success in the spiritual life.

An ascetic is indeed a person who forces himself to do that which is conducive to the growth and development of the spiritual life: he loves God and one's neighbor. He refrains from everything that is contrary to love for God and one's neighbor, that is, evil deeds.

Thus, we can see that a constant battle of good with evil takes place in the soul of an ascetic. In ascetical literature, this battle with evil is named "spiritual" or "unseen warfare." This is what constitutes the very essence of asceticism or spiritual life.

Asceticism is the one sure path to the alluring lighthouse of happiness which all people seek. Happiness, as life experience shows, is not outside of a man, where he mistakenly looks for it, but inside. Happiness lies in a peaceful state of soul, in serenity and internal calm, which come from internal satisfaction following victory over evil and the eradication of bad habits that tyrannize the soul. Sinful habits create chaos and disarray. Evil inclinations cannot be peaceful, calm and joyful. The only way to pacify the soul is by suppressing and eradicating bad habits through asceticism, an ascetic way of life.

This, then, is why asceticism is absolutely necessary for all people without exception: it is a common good, a common heritage. One who is a stranger to asceticism is his own enemy and deprives himself of a higher good: peace, a tranquil conscience, and joy in union with God, Who is the one source of true happiness for man.

CHAPTER 11

The Holy Fathers
on Combating the Passions

We have already established that all Christians, monks and laymen alike, are called into uncompromising battle with the evil dispositions of their heart, for it is from these evil dispositions in the heart that arise and emanate all evil deeds, all those offenses that darken man's life and make it truly hell. These evil dispositions of the heart, which every Christian must battle and eradicate, are called "passions" in the writings of the Holy Fathers.

However, to overcome and eradicate passions is not enough. In the place of eradicated passions it is necessary to firmly implant in the heart their opposite counterparts, the good dispositions of the soul that are called "virtues" by the Holy Fathers. Otherwise that will take place of which the Lord Jesus Christ warned in the parable of the demon that went out of a man and then brought with him seven other demons worse than himself. *When an unclean spirit goes out of a man, he goes through dry places, seeking rest, and finds none. Then he says, "I will return to my house from which I came." And when he comes, he finds it empty, swept, and put in order. Then he goes and takes with him seven other spirits more wicked than himself, and they enter and dwell there; and the last state of that man is worse than the first* (Matt 12:43–45).

Why is this so? Because spiritual nature, just as physical nature, abhors a vacuum. The soul of man cannot remain empty and devoid of everything. If passions have been eradicated, then the opposing virtues must immediately be planted in their stead. Otherwise, the passions will return and, not having received gratification for an extensive time, they will begin to torment the person even more intensely, as if seven demons had entered instead of one.

Thus, we can say that the essence of asceticism consists in the eradication of passions and the planting in their place of the opposing virtues.

But where do the passions in man come from? All of the Holy Fathers, teaching on the spiritual life, with one voice agree that the root and source of all the passions is egoism or self-love, that is, unreasonable, wrongful love towards oneself. Egoism or self-love gives rise to three principal passions, the three fundamental roots of all the other passions: love of pleasure, greed, and love of glory. These three principal passions are enumerated in the Holy Scripture by the Apostle and Evangelist John the Theologian who says, *Do not love the world or the things in the world. . . . For all that is in the world—the lust of the flesh, the lust of the eyes, and the pride of life—is not of the Father but is of the world* (1 John 2:15–16).

From these three principal passions in turn come the following eight passions: (1) gluttony, (2) fornication, (3) avarice, (4) anger, (5) sorrow, (6) despair, (7) vainglory, and (8) pride. These eight passions engender yet more and more passions, which then branch out into a multitude of diverse and subtle variations of each of these principal passions. All of these innumerable passions tyrannize and torment the human heart, never giving a person rest and causing him unbearable suffering, from which he loses spiritual peace, inner balance, and tranquility of conscience. He feels deeply unhappy, sometimes experiencing truly hellish torment, as if experiencing the onset of those torments that inevitably await all unrepentant sinners, that is, all those people who have given themselves over to the passions and who are entrapped by them. According to St John of Kronstadt's analogy, "the passions are concealed snakes that constantly gnaw at the heart of man and never give him rest."

The Holy Fathers, who themselves led a spiritual life and were attentive to their souls, observed and thoroughly studied all the subtleties of this age-old tragedy of the human heart afflicted with passions. Based upon their own experience and examination of the internal life of man, they developed an entire science of fighting the passions, a kind of therapeutic course for the ailing soul. Knowledge of this science, which bears the name "asceticism," comprises the most vital, most necessary lifetime task for every Christian who recognizes the urgent necessity of the battle with evil.

What are the principal techniques in this battle? All of the Holy Fathers unanimously advise us that we, first of all, take precautionary measures so as to not allow the passions to be conceived and take root in our hearts. A passion that has already been firmly established in the heart and made a kind of second nature in man is very hard to battle. To root it out and conquer it without God's grace-filled help is completely impossible. Therefore, it is necessary to keep vigilant, to attentively watch one's own heart, and not allow any passions to take root therein.

What are these precautionary measures that must be taken against the development of passions? These measures consist in the constant and intensive mental battle with the thoughts, or, according to the Holy Fathers, so-called suggestions. The Holy Fathers differentiate the following separate stages or steps in this battle: (1) initial suggestion, (2) acceptance, (3) consent, (4) captivity, and (5) passion.

At first, the conception of something appears in our mind: a person or a thing, or simply some thought that suddenly comes to mind. This is called a "suggestion." In and of itself a "suggestion" is not at all sinful, for it is impossible for man to keep his mind free of thoughts. Thoughts arise in man apart from his will. In *The Sayings of the Holy Fathers*, it is written how a brother came to Abba Poemen one day and said, "Abba, I have many thoughts and am in danger from them." The elder took him outside and said, "Open the collar of your robe and don't let any wind in!" "I can't do that," answered the brother. "If you can't do that," said the elder, "then you can't stop the flow of thoughts, but it is your work to resist them."

Thus, to guard oneself from the influx of thoughts or different imaginings that appear in our mind is impossible, but it is necessary to resist them, that is, to not let those that are bad, sinful, or that lead one into sin to remain and become entrenched. Here begins the second stage in our relation to thoughts, the so-called acceptance stage.

The Holy Fathers define "acceptance" as entering into conversation with thoughts that arise, or attending to them as to a guest who has come into our home. This stage may be either not sinful or already sinful, the beginning of sin.

If, having directed our attention to the thought, we see that it is not good, but rather evil, and that it is leading us to sin, and immediately take up arms against it and strive to promptly chase it out of our consciousness, then this second stage will be as sinless as the first stage. But if, having examined the thought, we see that it is bad and sinful but, nevertheless, retain it in our consciousness, relish it and sympathize with it, then thus begins the third stage, which is fully sinful, the so-called consent.

The Holy Fathers call "consent" the willing acceptance of a thought that has entered the soul or of an object that it has imagined. This takes place when someone begins to envisage how to act upon the suggestions of a thought towards which his soul has become favorably disposed, although his conscience tells him that it is not good, that it is sinful. The culpability of this third stage varies depending upon the spiritual stature of a person. If someone has already reached a significant spiritual state and has learned well how to discern thoughts and how to repel sinful thoughts, then this third stage is considerably sinful if he, through laziness and neglect, did not act to immediately drive away this evil thought. But if someone who is still inexperienced in spiritual warfare is tempted by an evil thought and then, understanding its sinfulness, nevertheless drives it out, calling upon God for help, it is excusable.

According to St Nil of Sorsk, some Holy Fathers differentiate between two types or two stages of consent that vary in degree of culpability. "When someone, though conquered in thought, is determined in the root of his mind, in the depth of his heart, not to commit a sin or an iniquity in deed—this is the first type of consent." The second type of consent, according to St Gregory of Sinai, consists in the following: "when someone willingly accepts thoughts sent from the enemy and, agreeing and fraternizing with them, is conquered by them to such a degree that he not only does not resist the passion but decides to do everything as it suggests, and does not carry out his decision in deed only because he does not find an opportune time or place, or for some other reason that prevents him from carrying out his intention." Such a condition of the soul is quite culpable and requires an interdiction in Holy Confession, that is, a Church *epitimia*.*

From this second stage of consent, it is already a quite natural and easy transition to the fourth stage, so-called captivity. If a soul has accepted an evil thought and is completely gripped and carried away by it, this is called "captivity." "'Captivity' is the automatic attraction of our heart towards the thought, or the constant allowance for it to dwell in ourselves, that is, uniting with it, which impairs our good disposition. The peaceful condition of our spirit, our inner harmony and normal emotional balance are disrupted." However, as in the stage of consent, there can be different degrees of "captivity"—greater or lesser. St Nil of Sorsk

---

Epitimia is sometimes translated as "penance." However, this does not convey the proper Orthodox meaning of the term. *Penance* connotes an understanding of payment for a transgression. *Epitimia* is understood to be "medicine," which heals one from the damage inflicted by the commission of the transgression. It is not payment for the crime, which God freely forgives when one truly repents.—Ed.

says, "In one case, when your mind is possessed by thoughts and it is involuntarily carried away by evil thoughts against your will, you can quickly, with God's help, control your mind and return it to yourself and to your activity. The second case is when the mind, buffeted and torn from its good disposition as though by storms and waves, and driven towards evil thoughts, is incapable of returning to a quiet and peaceful state." Here also the degree of culpability varies, depending upon how and under which circumstances the "captivity" took place.

The highest degree of "captivity" and the final stage of one's enslavement to sin are called "passion." Of this, St Nil says the following: "Passion is such tendency and such action that, having nestled for a long time in the soul, by means of habit turns into its nature, as it were." Often falling into one and the same sin, a person comes to the point where that sin becomes so habitual that he cannot and does not have the power to live without the constant gratification of his sinful inclination. This sin, having become habit and second nature in him, is called a "passion."

Thus, we can see from the above that man's falling into sin takes place in accordance with a certain consistent pattern. The first stage of sin is the stage of "suggestion," when sinful thoughts and suggestions enter unintentionally, by chance, and contrary to one's will into one's soul, either through the senses, the emotions or through the imagination. This is sinless and is only a possible prelude to sin. "Acceptance" is the reception of a "suggestion," paying heed to it, which is not always without sin. "Consent" is when the soul delights in the thought or image that has been presented; at this point, there is the danger of actually falling into sin by deed. The next stage is "captivity," when the soul is so strongly drawn to sin that the peaceful state of the soul is disturbed. Finally comes "passion," the long-term and habitual delight in sinful thoughts and feelings, and the committing of sin in actual deed. This is already complete slavery to sin, and the one who does not repent and drive out his passion will be subject to eternal torment. However, someone possessed by one or another passion begins to experience a foretaste of eternal torment already in this life and will not find inner peace. At this point a very intense and persistent battle and the special Grace of God is necessary in order to renounce a sin that has become second nature.

Where do our passions come from? Do we need to struggle with them? Perhaps they are natural for us?

Yes, they are natural for us. However, they are not natural for the ideal man as God created him and as he should be according to God's intention; they are natural for man's fallen nature, which has been corrupted by the sin of the forefathers. *For behold, I was conceived in wickedness, and in sins did my mother bear me,* says the psalmist King David (Ps 50:7). Therefore, the Holy Fathers say, "do not be disturbed, do not be puzzled when you see within yourself the action of a passion. When a passion arises, struggle against it and strive to restrain it and eradicate it with humility and prayer" (Abba Dorotheos, Homily 13).

What do we especially need to remember in the battle with the passions? "Every resistance to the demands of the passions weakens them; constant resistance to a passion dethrones it. On the other hand, the fondness for a passion strengthens it; the constant fondness for a passion enslaves the one that has become fond of it" (St Ignatius (Brianchaninov)).

The Christian's resistance to passions should extend even to the crucifixion of *the flesh with its passions and desires* (Gal 5:24). Even the great Apostle Paul says of himself, *But I discipline my body and bring it into subjection, lest, when I have preached to others, I myself should become disqualified* (1 Cor 9:27). A constant battle with passions, a desire to trample and stifle them is necessary, spiritual struggle is necessary. But it is not spiritual struggle that liberates a Christian from the rule of the passions: it is the right hand of the Most High that liberates him, the grace of the Holy Spirit. But be that as it may, the grace of the Holy Spirit is given not otherwise than in response to man's personal effort, personal spiritual struggle. This is why Christ the Saviour says, *Strive¹ to enter through the narrow gate* (Luke 13:24).

The eradication of passions instills peace in a person's soul and restores spiritual balance and divine harmony. However, one must not stop here. As the Holy Fathers say, man's soul, freed from passions, should not venture to remain free and empty, devoid of virtue. Otherwise, it is easy for the passions to return and begin to torment and tyrannize man even more vehemently, as the seven demons about which the Lord spoke in His parable. The opposing virtues must be immediately planted in place of eradicated passions. The Holy Fathers enumerate these virtues in the following order: (1) abstinence is opposed to gluttony, (2) chastity is opposed to fornication, (3) nonacquisitiveness is opposed to avarice, (4) meekness is opposed to anger, (5) blessed tears about one's sins are opposed to despair, (6) sobriety is opposed to sorrow, (7) humility is opposed to vanity, and (8) love is opposed to pride.

Where does the battle with passions and the instilling of the opposing virtues finally bring a person?

Scripture clearly tells us, and presents us the ultimate goal of our strivings. *Therefore you shall be perfect, just as your Father in heaven is perfect* (Matt 5:48). This is the final aim of the strivings of the Christian who is battling with his passions. The aim is to become God-like. You say that this is an unattainable ideal, but that is what makes it an ideal. An ideal can only be an ideal when it is unattainable. One can only endlessly strive towards it. This is what constitutes the greatness of the Christian ideal: it demands constant perfection; unending striving towards lofty, divine perfection.

But what is this perfection? What characteristics and traits does it have?

There is a clear indication of this in Scripture. Wishing to remind believers what the Lord expects of us, the Holy Apostle Paul writes: *For this is the will of God, your sanctification* (1 Thess 4:3). And the Apostle Peter testifies to this even more expressively, more powerfully, citing the words of God Himself, borrowed from the Old Testament: *Be holy, for I am holy* (1 Pet 1:16).

Thus, the Christian ideal, the perfection towards which we must strive, is sanctity, which is similar to the sanctity of God. It follows that the attainment of Divine sanctity is the aim of our life. God created us in order for us to be holy as He Himself is holy and so that we would delight in the communion of love with Him. From this we can see how far contemporary life is from what it should be according to God's design. Why is this? A deviation from this design took place when our forefathers fell into sin. Sin distanced people from God and, as a result, made them unhappy and incessantly suffering. The life of struggle and asceticism amends the evil that was the occasion of sin. It frees us from the oppression of sin and gives us again the possibility to set forth on the path leading to sanctity and communion with God.

Divine love, which desires our salvation, waits for us to set out upon that path of the life of asceticism, which alone is salvific. And only then will we return to God, where awaits us that all-encompassing and absolute moral contentment. A person's spirit unconsciously strives for such contentment throughout his entire life, calling it "happiness," and in vain seeks it on earth amidst corruptible and impermanent things. This is that heavenly blessedness which God has prepared for us as a reward and crowning glory for victory over evil in our ascetic life struggle. It is the final result of all of man's striving on earth; the complete and most perfect gratification of all of the highest noble desires and needs of man's spirit.

CHAPTER 12

❦

Pastoral Asceticism

Pastoral asceticism comprises the most essential branch of the science of pastoral theology. This concerns the personal life of the priest: how he must behave in order to be at the height of his calling and successfully carry his yoke of pastoral service.

The word *asceticism* should not scare anyone. Sometimes it is misinterpreted, instilling superstitious fear in some and driving others away. Asceticism is nothing other than a struggle with passions and exercise in virtues. Both of these are prescribed for all Christians: not only monks but also laity and, even more so, priests, who are called to such a high service that requires particular purity of heart, freedom from passions, and constant exercise of virtues. *The whole world lies under the sway of the wicked one* (1 John 5:19), says the Apostle John, and because a pastor is called to be *an example to the believers in word, in conduct, in love, in spirit, in faith, in purity* (1 Tim 4:12), then it is natural that he must, even more than laity, battle with passions and instill virtues in himself in order to serve as an example to his flock. This is demanded by the loftiness of the pastoral calling and for the success of pastoral activity. After all, according to

St John Chrysostom, God invested the priest with great power that He did not even give to angels nor archangels. Christ Himself emphasizes the differentiation of priests from the sinful, worldly environment when He says, *You are not of the world, but I chose you out of the world* (John 15:19).

Concerning this, the Righteous Father John of Kronstadt says, "What a great personage a priest is! He constantly converses with God, Who perpetually replies to his speech. Whatever the ceremonies of the Church may be, whatever his prayers, he is speaking to God, and the Lord answers him. How, under these circumstances, when assaulted by passions, can the priest forget that such passions are base, impure, especially for him, and that it is impossible to let them enter into his heart, which Jesus Christ alone ought to fill entirely? A priest is an angel and not a man; everything worldly ought to be left far away behind him. O Lord, *Thy priests shall be clothed with righteousness* (Ps 131:9); let them always remember the greatness of their calling and do not let them be entangled in the nets of the world and the Devil (*My Life in Christ*).

The frequent communing of the Holy Mysteries particularly obliges a priest to spiritual heights and constant, sober watchfulness over himself. If a long period of preparation is required of laity before they are allowed to commune, then how can a priest dare to come to the Holy Mysteries without fear and trembling, without dedicating his entire life to preparedness for frequent communion? Does not his entire existence need to be constant preparation, vigilant watchfulness over himself, perpetual cleansing of himself from every sinful defilement for readiness to commune of Christ's Holy Mysteries without judgment?

Having Christ in your heart, fear that you may lose Him, and with Him the peace in your heart; it is hard to begin again; efforts to attach oneself afresh to Him after falling away will be very grievous, and will cost bitter tears to many. Cling to Christ with all your might, gain Him, and do not lose boldness in approaching Him. (*My Life in Christ*)

This is why ascetic spiritual struggle is immensely significant for the priest. Pastoral asceticism should occupy the most important place in the science of pastoral theology, and should be its cornerstone. For it is clear to all that success in pastoral work depends upon the person of the pastor. The flock pays attention not so much to the priest's words or his teaching as to his private life, his conduct—whether or not he is worthy of his office. Where the priest is at the height of his calling, the flock is a beautiful example of true Christian life. There is no atheism, depravity, or sectarianism. On the contrary, in a parish where the priest is unworthy, all goes to ruin. In their search for a true example of religious and moral behavior, its members resort to all manner of sects. Woe to the pastor whose personal life is a poor example for his flock. The terrible words of Christ the Saviour apply to him: *It would be better for him if a millstone were hung around his neck, and he were drowned in the depth of the sea. Woe to the world because of offenses! For offenses must come, but woe to that man by whom the offense comes!* (Matt 18:6–7). A pastor behaving himself poorly takes upon his soul a sin much greater than a layman. When he does not attempt to change his sinful life, does not repent, he kills not only himself but also tempts many of his flock by his example. This is why there cannot be "worldly" pastors, but every pastor, both monastic and married, must be cut off from the world to a certain extent, must love ascetical struggle and practice it. Therefore, those who consider that an ascetical way of life is only the lot of monks and that the laity can live as they please are mistaken. It is a fallacy that only monastic clergy should strictly watch over themselves and that married clergy have the right to live unrestrainedly and in a worldly manner, not to wear a cassock and wander here and there according to the vain customs of this world. This is simply not true. St John Chrysostom speaks of the difference between monastics and laity: the only distinction is the vow of chastity. The other commandments are mandatory for all Christians.

What does pastoral asceticism consist of? It is the refusal of indulgence in even rightful pleasures so as to not inhibit the Gospel of Christ. The Holy Apostle Paul speaks about this (1 Cor 9). The principal activity of a pastor is the rejection of things worldly and the battle with passions in order to be the "light of the world"; *Let your light so shine before men, that they may see your good works and glorify your Father in heaven* (Matt 5:16).

NOTES

INTRODUCTION

1. The Russian word translated as "struggle" is подвиг [podvig].

CHAPTER 1

1. This is a reference to World War II (1939–1945).

CHAPTER 2

1. Quotes in this chapter from *The Spiritual Life and How to Be Attuned to It* by Bishop Theophan the Recluse were taken from the publication by St Paisius Monastery Press and used with permission.

CHAPTER 4

1. «Противобожественный фронт» Under the Soviet regime in Russia, religion was virulently assaulted by various groups, such as the League of Militant Atheists.—Ed.

2. Archbishop Averky had recently lived through the air raids and bombings of World War II.—Ed.

CHAPTER 6

1. From the Great Blessing of the Waters.—Trans.

2. Вонючую псинку is a play on words. Псинка [psinka] is a highly toxic weed, solanum nigrum, known in English as black nightshade or hound's berry. The word псинка is also the diminutive of псина, which means either "dog's flesh" or "dog's smell."—Ed.

3. Slogans of the Socialist-Revolutionary Party in Russia.—Ed.

4. The King James version translates this word as "heady."—Trans.

CHAPTER 7

1. See, for example, Matt 23:4.—Trans.

CHAPTER 8

1. A theomachist is one who battles or fights against God.

CHAPTER 11

1. Literally, "make spiritual struggle."—Trans.

SUBJECT INDEX

Citations in parentheses following page numbers refer to note numbers; for example, p. 52(n1) refers to the text associated with note 1 on page 52.

abstinence, 80, 135
"acceptance" stage, 130–131, 133
Adam, 2. *See also* first man
adversary, conscience as, 70
altruism, humanistic, 32–47
angels/archangels, 84, 139
anger, 22, 80, 81, 128, 135
animal egoism, 13, 41
animals
    bodies of, 21
    souls of, 19, 23
Anthony, Abba, 86
Antichrist, 1, 16, 17, 54
apocalyptic times, 17, 69
apostasy/apostates, 17, 103, 112–113

Apostles
    Christian struggle and, 124
    humility and, 6
    at Mystical Supper, 32
Arianism, 9
art, 11, 12, 92
asceticism/ascetic, ix–xxiv, 125–126
    for all Christians, x, xix, xxi, xxii, 126, 138
    conscience and, 68
    distorted view of, ix–xi, xiii, xix
    divine love and, 137
    essence of, x, xviii, 125, 128
    final goal of, xviii

asceticism/ascetic *(continued)*
  good works and, xiii
  Gospel love and, 33
  Greek roots of word,
    xiii–xiv, xix
  Greek word compared
    with Russian
    "struggling," xix,
    143(n1)
  and guarding the heart, 87
  happiness and, xxii
  holiness and, xxiii
  humility in, 9–10
  inner disposition and,
    xvii *(see also*
    disposition)
  meaning of "exercise"
    in, xiii–xiv
  modern/secular view of,
    ix–x, xiii, xix
  most important thing
    about, x
  pastoral, 138–141
  as science developed by
    Holy Fathers, 129
  spiritual life and, x, xi
    (see also spiritual
    life)
  spiritual training and,
    xiv–xv
  spiritual/unseen warfare
    in, 112 *(see also*
    spiritual/unseen
    warfare)
  struggle/battle involved
    in, xii, xiv–xv,
    xvii–xix *(see also*
    Christian struggle;
    struggle/battle)
  uniting man and God
    by, xxi–xxii
Atheists/atheism,
    51–52, 103, 113,
    140
"attention to oneself,"
    86–97, 129.
    See also guarding
    the heart
avarice, 135. *See also* greed

Basil the Great, St, 70
battle. *See* struggle/battle
body
  of animal, 21
  soul and, xiii, 18–23, 26
  soulless, 31
  spirit and, 19, 20, 23, 26
  will and, 22
brain, 22, 26
brutality, 64, 69, 81

"captivity" stage, 132–133, 134

carnality, 30, 51

Catholicism. *See* Roman Catholicism

charity, 43–44

chastity, 135, 141

children, 63, 87–88

Christian freedom, 80. *See also* freedom/ free will

Christianity/Christian religion

  art/science and, 11

  egoism *vs.*, 56

  heresies/schisms in, 9

  humanism *vs.*, 12

  joy in, 78–79

  paganism *vs.*, 8–9

  persecution and, 9

  science/art in, 11, 12

Christian love, 102, 106, 107. *See also* Gospel love

Christians

  asceticism for all, xix, xxi, xxii

  critics of, 36–37

  the first, 33, 68

  forgiveness and, 100

  laity *vs.* clergy among, 112–113

  light *vs.* darkness and, 110

  martyred, 8, 68

  modern, x, xix

  perfection and, 114–115

  and resisting evil, 99 *(see also* evil, resisting)

  as servants of God, 110

  as "soldiers," 110, 111

Christian struggle, 122–126. *See also* asceticism/ ascetic; spiritual/ unseen warfare; struggle/battle

  free will and, 122–123

  good works in, 123

  self-restraint and, 124–125

"Christians" without Christ, 36, 37

Church

  attendance at, 80, 113

  freedom and, 80

  and guarding the heart, 95

  heresies and, 9–11

  instructions/demands of, 80–81

  laity *vs.* clergy in, 113

Church *(continued)*
   and monks *vs.* laymen, xxi
   and resisting evil, 99, 105,
      106
   schisms in, 9–11
   sinful habits and, 78
   substitutes for, 27–28
cigarette smoking, 77–78,
      80, 144(n2)
combating passions, 127–137
   "acceptance" and, 130–
      131, 133
   "captivity" and, 132–133,
      134
   "consent" and, 131–132,
      133
   "passion" and, 133–135
   science of, 129
   "suggestion" and, 130,
      133
commandments, xii
   conscience and, 69
   free will and, 72–73
   Gospel love and, 38, 40,
      44–46, 50, 51, 54, 56
   greatest, 33–34, 37, 45
   new one, 32, 56
communion with God,
      xvii–xxiv, xix, 25,
      31, 136, 137, 139

communism, 13, 14, 15
compassion, 75, 107
confidence (in self), 116
conscience, 12–13, 24–25,
      61–70
   asceticism and, 126
   awakening too late of, 70
   chastisement by, 70
   in combating (sinful)
      passions, 131
   in first man (in paradise),
      73
   "freedom of," 82
   guarding one's, 68, 69
   and guarding the heart,
      89
   hardening of, 66–67, 69
   moral regression and, 62
   passions (sinful) and, 129
   pride and, 27
   stifled, 69
   and will of God, 66, 67,
      68
"consent" stage, 131–132,
      133
contemplation, in ascetism,
      xiv
corruption, 2, 3
   freedom and, 82
   Gospel love *vs.,* 44

corruption *(continued)*
  of man's nature, 134
creation, Gospel love and,
  32–33, 49
criminals, conscience and,
  63
Cross, 33, 35, 76
crucifixion
  of the flesh, 135
  of self, xiv–xv
cruelty, conscience and, 63,
  64

daydreaming, 96
death, 8, 59, 68
debauchery, 63, 80
deceit, 64, 116, 117
demons, 80, 81, 127–128,
  135
depravity, xvi, xvii, 3, 31, 140
  Gospel love and, 35
  humanism and, 12
  youth exposed to, 44
depression, Gospel love and,
  55
despair, 94, 120, 121, 136
destruction, 112
devil, 2, 72, 73–77, 139.
      See also slavery
      (to devil/sin)

discernment. *See* spiritual
  discernment
disciples, 1, 6, 46, 58, 60
  Holy Spirit sent to, 76
  at Mystical Supper, xii,
    32, 60
disposition, xvi–xviii, xvii,
    81. *See also* heart;
    passions (sinful);
    soul; virtue(s)
  impaired by "captivity,"
    132, 133
  predisposition, 57
  of society, 59
  spiritual/unseen warfare
    and, 115, 117, 123,
    127
  struggle/battle and,
    x, xii
distractions. *See* life
  distractions
divine contemplation, in
  ascetism, xiv
divine love/God's love, 33,
    49. *See also* Gospel
    love
  asceticism and, 137
  free will and, 71–72
  and resisting evil, 107
  response to, 71–72

divine revelation, 51.
     See also Revelation
     of God
divorce, conscience and, 63
Dorotheos, Abba, xx, 65–66,
     68, 112, 134

egoism/egotistical, 13
     Christian struggle and,
          124
     conscience and, 63, 64, 67
     Gospel love *vs.,* 35, 36–37,
          40, 41, 43, 47–50,
          56, 57
     happiness lacking in,
          54, 55
     natural love and, 56–57,
          58
     as source of passions
          (sinful), 128
emotions, 28–29, 49, 50
enmity, 80, 101, 102
entertainment, 30
     and guarding the heart,
          92, 94, 95–96
     youth and, 44
envy, 72, 80
evangelical love, xiii, xx
evil, 72. *See also* devil; evil
     habits/works;

     evil will; Satan;
          temptation; tree of
          knowledge of good
          and evil
     conscience and, 62,
          65, 66
     considered/disguised as
          good, 62, 81, 114
     forgiveness and, 100, 102
     freedom and, 82
     judgment of, in others,
          111
     life distractions and, 93,
          97
     resisting, 98–107, 130
     struggle/battle against,
          xii–xix, xxii, 99–100,
          110–121
evil habits/works. *See also*
          passions/sinful
          passions
     asceticism and, xvii
     Church and, xxi
     good works *vs.,* xii, xiii,
          xvi
     Gospel love and, 40
     inner disposition and,
          xvii
     monks and, xx
     spiritual training and, xiv

evil habits/works *(continued)*
    struggle/battle against,
        xiii, xvii, 110–121
evil will, xvi, xvii

faith
    Christianity and, 37
    good works and,
        xi–xii, 37, 39, 124
    Gospel love and, 34–35,
        55
    "in one's own god," 15–17
    "new," 15–17
    persecutors of the, 103
    in personal God, 27
    in self *vs.* God, 27
Fall of man/fallen state, 37,
        72–73
    Gospel love and, 49, 56
    passions (sinful) as
        natural to, 134
fasting, 80, 113
feast days, 113
feelings
    conscience and, 67
    psychology of, 22
first man, 72–73. *See also*
        Adam
flesh, xv, 12–13, 57
forgiveness, 100, 102–105

freedom/free will, 71–85.
      See also slavery
      (to devil/sin)
    Christian, 80, 81, 85
    Christian struggle and,
        122–123
    devil's envy of man's, 72
    example of, 78
    as gift from God, 71
    and guarding the heart,
        92
    holiness and, 114–115
    humility and, 7
    imaginary, 82, 84, 85
    life distractions and, 92
    meaning of, 72
    misuse of, 72
    modern conception of,
        79–83
    restored by Christ, 76, 77
    of spirit, 81
    true, 77, 80, 81, 85
    will of God and, 77

gluttony, 92, 135
God. *See also* Jesus Christ
    asceticism uniting man
        and, xxi–xxii
    belief in, 48–49
    as Benefactor, 38, 40, 49

God *(continued)*
  conscience as "voice of,"
      25
  as Creator, 49 (*see also*
      creation)
  faith in self *vs.* in, 27
  as Father, 38, 40, 49, 71,
      72, 76
  fear of, 24
  law of, xv, 63, 64, 103
  as mother, 49
  the One, 4, 15, 55, 119, 121
  personal, 27
  power of, 76
  spirit given by, 23, 24
  "Spirit of," 18
  thirst for, 24, 25
  union with, 126 (*see also*
      communion with
      God)
  voice of, 65
  will of (*see* Will of God)
  worship of, 116
God-like, 136
good. *See also* tree of
      knowledge of good
      and evil
  conscience and, 65, 66
  evil considered/disguised
      as, 81, 114

  before Fall of man, 73
  God as source of all, 117
  law of, xv
  "good for goodness' sake,"
      36, 37, 40, 42, 44
good will, xi, xvi, xvii
good works, xi–xii. *See also*
      love, works of
  asceticism and, xiii, xvii
  evil habits/works *vs.,* xii,
      xiii, xvi
  faith and, xi
  good will and, xi, xii,
      xvi, xvii
  Gospel love and, 38–39
  without faith in Christ,
      37, 39, 42–43
Gospel, 19
  criticism of, 53
  and guarding the heart,
      95
  pastoral asceticism and,
      141
  perfection as ideal in, 114
  and resisting evil, 98–99
  theomachists and, 52,
      144(n1)
Gospel love, 32–60. *See also*
      Christian love
  acquiring, 48–60

Gospel love *(continued)*
  natural love *vs.,* 55–58
  social charity *vs.,* 43–44
  substitutes for, 36, 55–56
governments
  conscience and, 64
  and resisting evil, 104
grace
  and battle against evil,
      xvii–xviii, 110, 115,
      117, 120–123 (*see
      also* spiritual/unseen
      warfare)
  and combating passions,
      134, 135
  of Holy Spirit, 76, 135
  humility and, 7
  pride and, 8, 116–117
  and slavery to sin, 134
greed, 128. *See also* avarice
Gregory of Sinai, St, 132
guarding the heart,
      86–97. *See also* life
      distractions
  children and, 87–88
  from harmful
      impressions, 88–90

happiness, xxii. *See also* joy
  asceticism and, 125, 126

freedom and, 79
and guarding the heart,
    87–88
moral contentment as,
    137
hatred, 32, 46, 53, 55, 56
  natural love and, 57, 59
  and slavery to sin, 80
heart, 22. *See also*
    disposition
  Gospel love and, 55, 56,
    60
  Guarding (*see* guarding
    the heart)
  Jesus Christ and priests',
    139, 140
  purity of, 87–88, 138
  passions (sinful) in,
    127–137
  virtuous *vs.* depraved,
    xvi, xvii
hell, 33, 39
  life comparable to, 15, 75,
    80, 111, 127
  in soul, 77
heresies, 9–11
holiness, xxiii
  Gospel love and, 35
  perfection as, 114, 136
Holy Church. *See* Church

154   *Subject Index*

Holy Fathers. *See also
        Sayings of the Holy
        Fathers*
    conscience and, 62, 67,
        68, 69
    and guarding the heart,
        86, 89, 90
    passions (sinful)
        (*see* passions/sinful
        passions)
    peace and, 102, 103
    science of fighting
        passions developed
        by, 129
    self-crucifixion and, xiv
    spiritual/unseen
        warfare and,
        115–118, 119
Holy Liturgy, 63
Holy Mysteries, 139
Holy Scripture. *See*
        Scripture
Holy Spirit, 76, 115
    and combating passions,
        135
    spiritual love and, 59
hope, 115, 120, 121
human beings/race. *See also*
        first man
    animals *vs.,* 21

devil "lord and master"
        of, 75, 76
    five senses of, 21, 89–90,
        91
humanism, 11–12
    altruism in, 32–47, 36, 43
    apostasy and, 112
    freedom and, 81–82
human rights, 83
human spirit, xxi. *See also*
        spirit
humility, 5–17
    and combating passions,
        134, 136
    God's strength as, 7
    Gospel love and, 54
    proud faith *vs.,* 17
    spiritual/unseen warfare
        and, 121
hypocrisy
    in advocacy of freedom,
        83
    conscience and, 64
    good works and, xvi

ideal, 25, 134, 136
idolization, 4, 12
Ignatius (Brianchaninov),
        St/Bishop, xvii, 50,
        51, 55–58

Ignatius (Brianchaninov)
(*continued*)
and combating passions,
135
conscience and, 66, 67
and guarding the heart,
90, 91, 93–94, 95, 96
infidelity, conscience and, 63
insensibility, 62, 68, 69
insignificance, one's own,
118–119
insolent people, 83, 144(n4)
Isaac the Syrian, St, xvii,
112, 118

Jesus Christ. *See also* Cross;
Sermon on the
Mount
call to spiritual life by, x,
110–111
Christian struggle and,
124
commandments of,
32, 34 (*see also*
commandments)
demoniac and, 80, 81
demons and, 127
Gospel of. *See* Gospel;
Gospel love
grace of, xvii–xviii

and guarding the heart,
86, 87–88, 90
as Head of Church, 70
Holy Mysteries of, 139
humility of, 5, 8, 17, 48, 54
law of, 13–14
life (soul) and, 19
as the Lord, 114, 117
on man's heart/inner
disposition, xvi
moneychangers' tables
and, 104
and monks *vs.* laymen,
xx–xxi
new commandment by, 32
as Only-Begotten Son, 4,
5, 32, 33, 48, 76, 119
and resisting evil, 101,
102, 104 (*see also*
spiritual/unseen
warfare)
resurrection of, 76
as Saviour, x, xvi, 1, 35,
39, 45, 49, 76–77, 86,
87–88, 98, 100, 140
as Son of God, 5, 9, 33,
34–35, 37, 47, 76
"spirit of," 6, 14, 17, 54
as Teacher of Love, 102,
104

Jesus Christ *(continued)*
  teaching of, 11, 37, 56, 77
  warnings by, 39, 40, 127
  on will of God, xxii–xxiii
John, St/Apostle/Evangelist/
    Theologian, 1, 38,
    40, 46, 128, 138
John Chrysostom, St, 117,
    139, 141
John of Kronstadt, St/
    Father, 80, 89–90,
    129, 139
John of the Ladder, St, 112
joy, 39, 40. *See also*
    happiness
  acesticism and, 125, 126
  freedom and, 78, 79, 80
  and guarding the heart,
    87–88
judge, conscience as, 65, 66

Kingdom of God, humility
    and, 6

laity/laymen
  clergy *vs.,* 112–113, 141
  monks and, 115, 127, 138,
    141
  priests and, 138, 140
law, natural, 66

law of God, xv, 63, 64, 103
law of sin, xv, xviii, xxixv,
    74. *See also* evil
    habits/works
  after Fall of man, 74
  Church and, xxi
laws of nature, miracles
    and, 52–53
League of Militant Atheists,
    52, 143(n1)
life, 8
  of body *vs.* soul, 23
  comparable to hell, 15,
    75, 80, 111, 127
  God's love and, 33, 59
  law of Christ and, 13–14
  "of struggle," xix
  soul and, 18–19, 21
life distractions, 86–97,
    144(n1). *See also*
    guarding the heart
  harm in, 91, 93
  results of, 93–94
  warned against, 90–91
Lord, the. *See* Jesus Christ
Lord's Prayer, 100
love. *See also* Christian love;
    Gospel love
  evangelical, xii
  of glory, 128

love *(continued)*
    God's (*see* divine love/
        God's love)
    natural, 55–58
    of pleasure, 128
    of power, 80
    pride *vs.,* 136
    and resisting evil, 102, 106
    self-love, 35, 48, 115, 128
    spiritual, 59
    Teacher of, 102, 104
love for God, xii, xiii, xv–
        xvi, xviii, 34,
        43, 44. *See also*
        Gospel love
    acquiring, 49
    asceticism and, 125
    emotions and, 49, 50
    free will and, 71
    litmus test for, 46
love for neighbor, xiii, xv–
        xvi, xviii, xx, 34, 43,
        44, 46
    asceticism and, 125
    conscience and, 69
    joy in, 54–55
    life distractions and,
        93–94, 144(n1)
    as measure of love for
        God, 54

natural *vs.* Gospel, 57, 58
    (*see also* Gospel love)
substitutes for, 55–56
lust, 91–92

malice, 55, 56, 59
martyrs, 8, 68
materialism, 13, 26, 30
maternal love, 57–58
mercy, 5, 17, 39, 43
mind, conscience and, 66,
    67, 75
miracles, 52–53
modern Christians, x, xix
modern/secular view, x, xix.
    See also secular life/
    world
    of asceticism, ix–x, xiii,
        xix
    of freedom, 79–83
    and guarding the heart,
        92
    spiritual *vs.,* xi, 29–30, 31,
        113–114
monks/monastics, xiv, xix
    laity and, 115, 127, 138,
        141
    laity *vs.,* xx–xxi, 113
morality
    conscience and, 65

morality *(continued)*
    Gospel love as foundation
        for, 46
    "independent," 43, 44
    motive for Christian, 49
    and slavery *vs.* freedom,
        82–83
    without Gospel love/
        religion, 36, 37,
        39–42
moral perfection, freedom
    and, 77
murder, 80, 103, 106
music, 28–29
My Life in Christ, 90, 139,
    140
Mystical Supper, 6, 32, 60

natural law, 66
nature, asceticism and, xxi
neighbor. *See* love for
        neighbor
"new faith," 15, 16
Nil of Sorsk, St, 131, 132–133
Noah, 3, 31

obedience, 8, 12
    conscience and, 71, 73
    free will and, 71
    Gospel love and, 45–46

Old Testament, 33, 101, 136
Only-Begotten Son. *See*
        Jesus Christ

paganism, 4, 8–9, 10
paradise, 15, 69, 73
parents
    conscience and, 63
    youth exposed to
        depravity by, 44
passions/ sinful passions,
        77–78, 80, 81,
        127–137. *See also*
        evil habits/works
    as defined by Holy
        Fathers, 133, 134
    and guarding the heart,
        87
    list of, 128
    pastoral asceticism and,
        138, 141
    precautionary measures
        against, 130
    pride and, 116
    priests and, 138, 139
    spiritual/unseen warfare
        against, 115, 121
    virtues replacing, 128,
        135
pastoral asceticism, 138–141

pastoral theology, 138, 140
paternal love, 57–58
Paul, St/Apostle, xi, xiv, 4,
17
conscience and, 66, 74
God's strength and, 7
humility and, 6–7
pastoral asceticism and,
141
sanctification and, xxiii,
136
Satan and, 26
self-crucifixion and,
xiv–xv, 135
soul *vs.* spirit and, 19
peace
asceticism and, 125, 126
"captivity" and, 132, 133
of Christ, 60, 102
and combating passions,
125, 126, 132–135
freedom and, 78, 80
"good," 102
Gospel love and, 59–60
and guarding the heart,
87–88
passions (sinful) and, 129
and resisting evil,
102, 103
penance, *epitimia vs.,* 132(n)

perfection, xxiii, 114, 136
Peter, St/Apostle, 83–84, 114
phariseeism, 38–39
philanthropy, 36, 41, 42, 43
philosophy, 27, 55
physical senses, 21, 89–91,
96–97
pleasure
love of, 128
pastoral asceticism and,
141
Poemen the Great,
St/Abba, 90, 130
politics, 55, 61, 64
power
of Christ, 76
of God, 7–8, 76
love of, 80
over the devil, 76
prayer, 80, 113, 115, 116,
118, 120–121
and combating passions,
134
natural state *vs.* spiritual,
28
of priest, 139
for realization of
weakness, 118
pride, self-asserting, 2–17
conscience and, 67

pride *(continued)*
  and faith in self *vs.* God, 27
  forgiveness and, 103, 104
  Gospel love *vs.,* 35–36, 44,
      48–50, 50, 54
  heresies resulting from, 9
  humanism and, 12, 13
  humility *vs.,* 5–17
  hymn to, 16
  as idol, 116
  love *vs.,* 136
  masquerade of, 25–26
  national pride as, 3
  paganism and, 4
  in Protestantism, 11
  and resisting evil, 101
  Satan and, 25–26
  and slavery *vs.* freedom,
      79, 80, 83
  spiritual/unseen warfare
      and, 115, 116, 118
  in Western Roman
      Church, 10
priests, 61
  as example to flock, 138
  laity and, 115, 138
  pastoral asceticism and,
      138–141
Protestantism, 10, 11, 123,
    124

Providence, 52, 53
psychology, 22, 26
purity of heart, 87–88, 138

reason
  conscience and, 67
  cult of, 12
recluse, asceticism and, xiv
religion, 114, 142
  morality independent of,
      36, 37
  national character in, 4
  philosophy *vs.* authentic,
      27
  true, 39, 55
Renaissance, 11–12, 36
repentance, 5
  conscience and, 62, 63,
      68, 70
  Gospel love and, 51
  spiritual/unseen warfare
      and, 120, 121
rewards/punishments,
      39, 40, 66. *See also*
      chastisement
righteousness, 88, 110
Roman Catholicism, 10, 11,
      40, 124
rulers, conscience and,
      64–65

Russia, 28, 43, 52, 79,
        143(n1), 144(n3)

salvation, xxiv, 17, 31, 70,
        137
sanctification, xxiii, 35, 136,
        137
Satan
    as angel of light, 26
    Apostle Paul and, 7
    and guarding the heart, 92
    pride and, 25–26
    warfare against, 110, 118
        (*see also* spiritual/
        unseen warfare)
Saviour. *See* Jesus Christ
Sayings of the Holy Fathers,
        86, 130
schisms, 9–11
science, 11, 12, 22
    conscience and, 67
    miracles and, 52–53
    of pastoral theology, 138,
        140
Scripture, 90, 104, 120, 123,
        128, 554
    perfection in, 114, 126, 136
    Protestantism and, 11,
        124
    soul *vs.* spirit in, 20

sectarianism, 140
sects, 10, 11, 140
secular life/world. *See also*
        modern/secular view
    asceticism as viewed by,
        ix–x, xiii
    conscience and, 62–63
    laity *vs.* clergy in, 113, 115
    science/art and, 12
self-asserting pride. *See*
        pride, self-asserting
self-centeredness, 115, 116
self-crucifixion, xiv–xv
self-deceit, 116, 117
self-love, 35, 48, 115, 128
self-restraint, x, 122,
        124–125
Sermon on the Mount,
        xxii–xxiii, 5–6, 98,
        123–124
sin, xxiii. *See also* evil habits/
        works; Fall of man/
        fallen state; slavery
        (to devil/sin)
    of Adam and Eve, 2
    asceticism and, 137
    battle against
        (*see* spiritual/unseen
        warfare; struggle/
        battle)

sin *(continued)*
  conscience and, 63, 66, 67, 73
  corruption and, 2, 3
  falling into, 118, 120, 121, 133–134
  forgiveness of, 5
  freedom and, 79, 80
  good will *vs.,* xi
  Gospel love and, 35, 45, 50
  grace and, xi
  holiness *vs.,* xxiii
  humanism and, 12
  law of, xviii, xxixv, 74
  tyranny of, 80
situational ethics, 36
slander, 64, 72
slavery (to devil/sin), 72, 73–77, 82, 84. *See also* freedom/ free will
  combating passions and, 134
  modern life and, 79–83
"social injustice/ills," 13, 14
socialism, 13, 14, 15
society
  conscience and, 63–64
  disposition of, 59
  suppressing evil in, 104, 105
Son of God. *See* Jesus Christ
sorrow(s), 156
  Gospel love and, 46
  life distractions and, 94
  spiritual/unseen warfare and, 118, 120, 121
soul, xviii–xix. *See also* disposition; heart
  of animals, 18, 23
  battle in, xii, 111–112, 113–114, 125 (*see also* evil, resisting; evil habits/ works; spiritual/ unseen warfare)
  body and, 18–21, 22–23
  brain and, 22
  as "bridge" from body to spirit, 20
  combining of spirit with, 26, 27
  conscience and, 24, 65, 66, 69
  evil in, 14–15
  freedom and, 77, 85
  good *vs.* evil will of, xvi
  joy/peace in, 78, 125, 126
  life and, 18–19, 21

soul (*continued*)

    parts of, 21–22

    spirit combined with, 26, 27

    and Spirit of God, 18

    spirit *vs.,* 19, 20, 23

    "windows of the," 88–89

spirit

    of Antichrist, 17

    asceticism for human, xxi

    body *vs.,* 19, 20, 23

    of Christ, 54

    conscience and, 65, 66

    divine origin of, 23, 24

    existence of, rejected/ ignored, 26–27

    flesh *vs.,* 12–13

    freedom of, 81

    moral contentment and, 137

    needs of, substitutes for, 27–28

    revealing of, 24–25

    soul combined with, 26, 27

    soul *vs.,* 19, 20, 23

    striving/yearning of, for God, 27

"spirit of Christ," 6, 14, 17

"Spirit of God," 18

spiritual discernment, 18–31

spiritual life

    asceticism and, x, xi, xiii, xvii, xviii, xxi (*see also* struggle/battle)

    authentic, 26, 27

    emotions and, 28–29

    essence of, 110, 125 (*see also* spiritual/ unseen warfare)

    flesh *vs.,* 12–13

    and guarding the heart, 88, 95

    modern life/society and, xi, 29–30, 31

    and monks *vs.* laymen, xxi

    science of (*askesis*), xiii

Spiritual Life and How to Be Attuned to It, The, 20, 23, 143(n1)

spiritual love, 49, 50, 59

spiritual/unseen warfare, xviii, 108–121, 122, 125. *See also* Christian struggle; struggle/battle

    example of one inexperienced in, 131

    monks and, xx

    visible *vs.,* 113–114

"stony insensibility," 62, 69
struggle/battle, xii, xiv–
        xv, 137. *See also*
        Christian struggle;
        spiritual/unseen
        warfare
    conscience and, 66, 74
    defeats in, xviii
    against evil, xii–xix, xxii,
        99–100, 110–121
    "for existence," 79,
        144(n3)
    grace in response
        to, 135
    and guarding the heart,
        88
    Holy Fathers and,
        127–137
    pastoral asceticism and,
        141
    of priests, 140
    and resisting evil, 102
"suggestion" stage, 130, 133
suicide, 94
Symeon, St/New
        Theologian, 75, 77,
        112

temptation, after Fall of
        man, 74–75

theomachists, 52, 103,
        144(n1)
Theophan the Recluse,
        St, 20, 23, 48, 66,
        143(n1)
thieves, 103, 106, 107
Tolstoy, Leo, 98, 99, 104
transgressions, 51, 63
tree of knowledge of good
        and evil, 73

vanity, 41–42, 136
vice
    conscience and virtue *vs.*,
        68
    freedom and, 77
    pride and, 116
    spiritual/unseen warfare
        against, 115
virtue(s), 43
    conscience and vice *vs.*, 68
    Gospel love and, 51
    heart/inner disposition
        and, xvi
    joy and, 79
    list of, 135–136
    passions (sinful)
        replaced by, 128, 135
    spiritual/unseen warfare
        for, 114, 123

war. *See also* spiritual/
    unseen warfare
  conscience and, 64
  pride and, 3–4
  and slavery to sin, 80
  for suppression of evil,
    106
weakness, 116–120
Western Roman Church,
    10, 11
wickedness, 32, 46, 47
will
  conscience and, 66, 67
  evil, xvi, xvii
  free (*see* freedom/free will)

  psychology of, 22
  self-will, 70
will of God, xxii, xxiii, 25,
    31, 45
  conscience and, 68, 73
"worldly" people/thinking,
    27–28, 31, 141
worship, 47
  of false gods, 4
  of pride instead of God,
    116

youth
  depravity and, 44
  pride and, 17

SCRIPTURE INDEX

Citations in parentheses following page numbers refer to note numbers; for example, p. 93(n1) refers to the text associated with note 1 on page 93.

Acts 14:22, p. 124

1 Corinthians 2:2, p. 17
1 Corinthians 2:14, p. 18
1 Corinthians 9, p. 141
1 Corinthians 9:24-27, p. xiv
1 Corinthians 9:27, p. 135
2 Corinthians 6:14-15, p. 110
2 Corinthians 12:9, pp. 7, 9, 115

Ephesians 2:10, p. xi

Galatians 5:15, p. 113
Galatians 5:24, p. xiv, 135
Galatians 6:2, p. 13
Genesis 1:20–24, p. 19

Genesis 1:24, p. 23
Genesis 2:7, pp. 19, 21
Genesis 3:1–7, p. 2
Genesis 3:19, p. 21
Genesis 6:3, p. 31

Hebrews 4:12, p. 20

Isaiah 5:21, p. 117

James 1:26–27, p. 39
James 2:26, p. xi
Jeremiah 6:13, 15, p. 60
Jeremiah 6:14, p. 60
1 John 2:2, p. 40
1 John 2:15–16, p. 128
1 John 2:16, p. 92

1 John 3:16, p. 38
1 John 3:23, p. 38
1 John 4:1–3, p. 1
1 John 4:3, p. 14
1 John 4:10–11, p. 40
1 John 4:16, p. 32
1 John 4:19, p. 40
1 John 4:20, pp. 40, 46, 54
1 John 4:21, p. 40
1 John 5:3, p. 40
1 John 5:19, pp. 87, 138
John 3:17, p. 46
John 3:18, p. 46
John 4:11, p. 46
John 8:31–32, p. 76
John 8:32, p. 71
John 8:33–36, p. 76
John 13:12–15, p. 6
John 13:34–35, p. 32
John 13:35, p. 46
John 14:15, pp. xii, 38, 50
John 14:24, p. 50
John 14:27, pp. 60, 102
John 15:19, p. 139
Jude 1:19, p. 19

Leviticus 19:2, p. 114
Luke 3:14, p. 106
Luke 6: 31, p. 14
Luke 8:28, p. 80

Luke 9:58, p. 5
Luke 13:24, p. 135

Mark 8:35, p. 19
Mark 12:31, p. 14
Mark 13:37, p. 90
Matthew 4:17, pp. 5, 70
Matthew 5:3, p. 5
Matthew 5:16, p. 141
Matthew 5:25–26, p. 70
Matthew 5:38–42, p. 98
Matthew 5:39, p. 101
Matthew 5:48, pp. xxiii,
      114, 136
Matthew 6:14–15, p. 109
Matthew 7:13–14, p. 124
Matthew 7:21, pp. xii, 124
Matthew 10:34, p. 102
Matthew 10:34–36, p. 57
Matthew 11:12, p. 124
Matthew 11:29, p. 6
Matthew 12:43–45, p. 128
Matthew 12:47–50, p. 58
Matthew 15:18–19, p. xvi
Matthew 15:19, p. 86
Matthew 16:6, p. 39
Matthew 18:1–3, p. 6
Matthew 18:3, p. 88
Matthew 18:6–7, p. 140
Matthew 20:26, pp. 6, 10

Matthew 22:37–49, p. 33
Matthew 22:41–46, p. 34
Matthew 23:4, p. 144(n1)
Matthew 24:12, p. 63
Matthew 26:41, p. 90

1 Peter 1:16, pp. xxiii,
    136
2 Peter 2:9–19, p. 84
Philippians 2:5, p. 6
Philippians 2:6–8, p. 7
Philippians 2:7, p. 76
Psalms 50:7, p. 134
Psalms 73:22, p. 30
Psalms 131:9, p. 139

Romans 1:28–31, p. 4
Romans 7:15–24, p. 74
Romans 7:18–25, p. xiv
Romans 7:23, p. 74
Romans 12:16, p. 117
Romans 13:1–4, p. 105
Romans 14:17, p. 88
Romans 15:1, p. 14

Sirach 2:10, p. 120

1 Thessalonians 4:3,
        pp. xxiii, 136
1 Timothy 4:12, p. 138
2 Timothy 3:4, p. 83